"With admirable clarity and precision, Markus Lundström outlines the key ideas of anarchism and uses them as a lens through which to analyze popular struggle. By pivoting his argument on the notion of the impossible, he explores the inherent tensions at the heart of democracy. This little book is a great introduction to anarchist thinking about politics and a powerful examination of popular dissent."
—Iwona Janicka, author of *Theorizing Contemporary Anarchism: Solidarity, Mimesis and Radical Social Change*

"This book addresses the confusions and ambiguities about the values that we claim for our collective lives when we employ the term 'democracy.' Never has this been a more urgent task as the world accelerates into social, economic, and environmental chaos, apparently regardless of the will of populations living in proclaimed democracies. How can we understand and move beyond these experiences of 'deprived political influence'? Lundström employs insights developed by anarchist writers and activists, particularly concerning domination, resistance, and conflict, to offer some clarity about these experiences. In this book, he helps us to think beyond the boundaries of the democratic tradition (where necessary) so that we can decide for ourselves which ways of life are possible and which we would like to make impossible."
—Carissa Honeywell, author of *Anarchism*

"In a nuanced, incisive, and admirably inclusive account of classical and contemporary anarchist thought, Lundström makes the Impossible Argument plausible. The critique of repressive and punitive authority must be in productive dialogue with the struggle to build non-hierarchical democratic relations if we are to sustainably change what 'democracy' looks like. Radical democratic thinking and action are vital in confronting the challenges of our times—the undermining of extractive and exploitative relations and the promotion of flourishing for all communities, human and not."
—Erika Cudworth, coauthor, with Steve Hobden, of *The Emancipatory Project of Posthumanism*

T0125694

"Lundström convincingly argues that the aporias of democracy are best explored within the anarchist tradition, which has always had an ambivalent attitude to democracy: what he calls the 'Impossible Argument.' In drawing on the theoretical resources of nineteenth- and twentieth-century anarchism, as well as empirical research from the site of contemporary struggles against the state, Lundström effectively illustrates the central tensions of democracy, developing from this new way of thinking about radical democracy in the twenty-first century."
—Saul Newman, author of *Postanarchism*

"It is easy to dismiss rioting youth as hooligans engaging in senseless violence. It is much more difficult but also much more rewarding to see them as political actors challenging formal frameworks of governance. Luckily, Lundström has stepped up to the task."
—Gabriel Kuhn, author of *All Power to the Councils! A Documentary History of the German Revolution of 1918–1919*

"The very best and most fruitful interrogations of political life often come from a deep and scrupulous plunge into a single event. So it is with Markus Lundström's brilliant analysis of the battle in the streets of Husby in 2013. The result is a subtle, philosophically informed, and original understanding of the possibilities for enacting the promise of anarchism."
—James Scott, author of *The Art of Not Being Governed: An Anarchist History of Upland Southeast Asia*

Anarchist Critique of Radical Democracy

The Impossible Argument

Markus Lundström

Anarchist Critique of Radical Democracy: The Impossible Argument
Markus Lundström © 2023
This edition © PM Press

ISBN: 978–1–62963–998–7 (paperback)
ISBN: 978–1–62963–999–4 (ebook)

Library of Congress Control Number: 2022943206

Cover design by John Yates/www.stealworks.com
Interior design by briandesign

10 9 8 7 6 5 4 3 2 1

PM Press
PO Box 23912
Oakland, CA 94623
www.pmpress.org

Printed in the USA

Contents

to the ungovernable

Preface to the
Second Edition

In the spring of 2013, massive protests against the police swept across Sweden. The spark was, as so often, a police shooting. An elderly man had been shot in his home, and the police tried to cover up the incident. Lenine Relvas-Martins was a sixty-nine-year-old community member of Husby, a marginalized city district in Stockholm that for years had put up with state-led mistreatment. Following the death of Relvas-Martins, Husby residents organized a demonstration to protest against police violence. Their demands for an official apology were ignored. One week after the killing, groups of people began to tackle police violence with other methods. During some intense May nights, violent confrontations between police and their adversaries in Husby triggered anti-police riots that soon spread to other cities across Sweden. Police cars, police stations, and police officers were attacked. In response, the state launched one of the fiercest police interventions in Swedish history; on the streets of Husby, people of all stripes were beaten, assaulted, humiliated, and violently racialized.

These painful experiences will no doubt linger in Husby's collective memory. In official discourse, however, they seem to be forgotten. When anti-police mobilization exploded in the 2020s US, following a series of racist police killings, demonstrations were held in Sweden in solidarity with Black Lives Matter. As political commentators debated racist police violence and anti-police demonstrations in Swedish mass media, not a single reference was made to the local anti-police riots that had taken place only a few years earlier. With a remarkably short memory, social mobilization in the US was generally portrayed as a *struggle for* democracy, whereas the Husby riots of 2013 had been described as an overall *threat to* democracy. That precise ambiguity is the theme of this book. We will revisit the 2013 anti-police riots in Sweden against a backdrop of democratic failure. We will then venture into an ideological tradition generically resistant to governance, namely, anarchism—with the overall aim being to spotlight ongoing searches for a more radical democracy.

My motivation for writing this book comes partly from personal encounters with state violence. Though comparably mild, these experiences awoke in me an urge to understand and to study the very nature of domination. That voyage took me deep into the political tradition that struggles for nothing less than to make every form of domination impossible. While studying the history of anarchist thought, I began to notice vivid ungovernable weeds of resistance sprouting even in the most democratic of environments. When listening to the people of Husby, I glimpsed into the depths of that complex collective experience. By reading radical democratic theorists, not least Jacques Rancière, I found tools to identify social antagonism within these experiences: the division between democratic government and those it tries to govern. That antagonism of democracy is at the heart of this updated edition of *Anarchist Critique of Radical Democracy: The Impossible Argument*.

The Search for Radical Democracy

My first encounter with a large-scale rally as an active participant was in December 2009. I was one of about a hundred thousand people who had gathered in Copenhagen to demonstrate and draw attention to the urgency of the political-ecological issues so obviously ignored by the governors of our democratic nation-states; we wanted more people to act as if our world(s) mattered. At the 2009 United Nations Climate Change Conference—the Copenhagen Summit—international cooperation again proved unable to deal with the severe threat of environmental degradation. In the shadow of that intense presence of global governance, I was introduced to ungovernable resistance enacted amid apparent powerlessness.

A few blocks down the march road, I saw police break into the demonstration, blocking both the way forward and the way back. A certain segment of the rally, about a thousand individuals, had been contained, since we apparently represented, as the police repeatedly told us, "the problematic part of the demo." Perhaps that was not incorrect. Some of us were, indeed, masked and dressed in black, confirming the iconic imagery of anarchist troublemakers, and many would certainly pay tribute to the enduring anarchist tradition. As we were sitting there, hour after hour, in temporary (and even, as it later turned out, illegal) confinement, people began chanting, cunningly, the very characteristic call-and-response of the late alterglobalization movement: "show me what democracy looks like!" and "this is what democracy looks like!"

Echoing between the walls in the twilight of midwinter Copenhagen, the chant delivered a rather cynical subtitle to that confined part of the rally. As a sarcastic reference to the leitmotif associated with the acclaimed "nonproblematic" part of the demo, the chant asserted, when coming from our restrained black bloc, an anarchist *critique* of democracy.

The aim of this book is to trace the genealogy of that critical thought, to expose and theorize a social conflict embedded in democracy itself: the antagonism between the government and those it tries to govern. The starting point for this exploration derives not from the self-identified anarchist milieu but from the collective experiences of democratic social conflict in Husby, a Stockholm city district located at Sweden's sociopolitical periphery. In the Swedish spring of 2013, a series of anti-police riots started in Husby and eventually spread throughout the country, challenging the image of Sweden as a peaceful and inclusive state of democracy. The social antagonism culminated in what became known as the Husby riots, which triggered one of the fiercest police interventions in Swedish history.

This book shows what democracy can look like when political activities are ignored and suppressed by municipal and state governors. In this sense, the Husby case exposes the conflictual nature of democracy, a conception that is central to ongoing scholarly theorizations and pursuit of a more *radical* democracy. Our inquiry into conflictual democratic antagonism will be guided by the radical democratic theory of Jacques Rancière, exposing an antagonism between the democratic life of the Husby community and the ignorant and repressive response of the democratic state. We will also see how these collective experiences include resistance struggles to remain ungovernable. The book digs deeper into this resistance phenomenon—the experiential critique of the democratic state—by exploring a political ideology targeting that very antagonism. In the historical tradition of anarchism, we will trace critical approaches to democracy in relation to anarchy. As we shall see, this ideological tradition not only defies the social divide between governors and governed but also nurtures a critique of democratic radicalization. This book aims to connect that anarchist critique, that Impossible Argument, to ongoing struggles for a more radical democracy.

Today's search for radical democracy is, of course, closely linked to the discursive centrality of the concept itself: actors across the political spectrum situate their projects in a democratic framework. We recognize "anti-democratic" and "nondemocratic" as pejorative ascriptions reserved for political adversaries. For the modern nation-state, it appears rather difficult—if not impossible—to pose as anything other than democracy. The same could certainly be said for nongovernmental organizations, social movements, and other agents of civil society. For state and nonstate actors alike, appropriating democracy to attain legitimacy appears to be at the very center of political action.

Ever since the concept became a subject for the scholarly community, most notably through the writings of the political economist Joseph Schumpeter,[1] it has been specifically defined by the procedural nature of political representation. Though widely debated throughout the twentieth century, democratic theory produced in the Global North typically denotes democracy as a certain political condition,[2] which, as Robert Dahl declares, is particularly apt for large-scale nation-states.[3] Democratic theory has been, as it were, the tonality of potential, of promising opportunity, indexed by a vigorous civil society.[4] After the collapse of state socialism in the early 1990s, left-leaning academic scholars soon began theoretical explorations to answer, in the words of David Trend, democracy's crisis of meaning.[5]

A strong current in that reconceptualization is this notion of *radical democracy*, construed as a path beyond both liberal and communitarian forms of democracy.[6] The adjective "radical" denotes the etymological root of democracy, people's rule, which evokes, as Chantal Mouffe puts it, "extension and deepening of the democratic revolution initiated two hundred years ago...a radicalization of the modern democratic tradition."[7] The connotations of radical democracy also encompass a pluralist feature, a theory of difference, heterogeneity, and social antagonism. This pluralist nature of democracy answers to the theory of deliberative democracy, most famously promoted by Jürgen Habermas, which presumes, or at least aims at, overall political consensus.[8] The universalist feature of this democratic theory is challenged in Ernesto Laclau and Chantal Mouffe's now classic book *Hegemony and Socialist Strategy*, which asserts political dissensus, or pluralism, as a key pillar of radical democracy.[9] For some time, the academic literature has been defined by the divide between the Habermasian interpretation and this post-Marxist interpretation,[10] though it is probably fair to say that most scholars now associate radical democracy with a contentious societal process.[11]

At the same time, the search for radical democracy is also catalyzed by an unblemished political inclination, the age-old dream of envisioning "the people" actually taking over the state apparatus. Douglas Lummis contends that "radical democracy is even more frightening than anarchism…[as it] does not abolish power, it says that the people should have it."[12] Indeed loyal to the Marxian tradition, though in the vein of reasserting Gramsci's notion of hegemony, Laclau and Mouffe declare that the "socialist strategy" ultimately crystallizes in "the people" taking over state power; the *demos* is to become re-invoked, in the words of Ernesto Laclau, as "the central protagonist of politics."[13] This elevation of so-called *left populism*, continuously endorsed by Chantal Mouffe, "presupposes allegiance to the political principles of modern democracy and the commitment to defend its key institutions."[14] From this theoretical perspective, which permits unity and autonomy as tandem political goals,[15] radical democratic pluralism validates through its materializations—and this in precisely the state arena. Following this line of thought, Mouffe distinctly warns about "exodus theorists," scholars—and radical movements—inclined, as Mouffe sees it, to withdraw from existing political institutions, thereby paving the way for a continued neoliberal rule.[16] In place of such a "total rejection of representative democracy," Mouffe suggests that "the state and representative institutions, instead of being an obstacle to social change, can contribute to it in a crucial way."[17]

Mouffe's alarmist reading of "beyond state politics" highlights her understanding of radical democracy as a left populist project to "radicalize democratic institutions and establish a new hegemony."[18] This defense of state politics answers largely to explorations of democracy within the alterglobalization movement in the Global North. According to Marianne Maeckelbergh, democracy within this movement is typically understood as "a non-state democracy, for some actors an anti-state democracy."[19] Maeckelbergh observes that in this sense democracy is "intentionally prefigurative," attempting to reinvent democracy beyond the state by creating, in the words of David Graeber, "viable models of what functioning direct democracy could actually look like."[20] Here we recall our anarchist critique of radical democracy, displayed by the sarcastic chant "this is what democracy looks like," echoing during heavy police repression at the Copenhagen summit. It is precisely this political inclination—to avoid or bypass the state political arena—that has startled radical theory scholars like Chantal Mouffe. In this vein, Barbara Epstein expresses unease at avoiding state politics, since "standing aside from this arena means leaving it to the right."[21] So also has Judith Butler, read as an advocate for radical democracy, been sharply criticized for disqualifying the state arena.[22]

In between these troubled discussions concerning the political imperatives of radical democracy dwells the theorization of democracy's conflictual nature. Mouffe famously diagnoses politics as *agonistic* instead of antagonistic; (radical) democracy is an arena for constant negation and social friction rather than an enforced factory for political consensus.[23] In the same vein, Laclau construes radical democracy as "the impossibility of mastering the contingent forms in which it crystallizes."[24] This line of thought draws on select writings of Karl Marx to reactivate, as Simon Critchley points out, "the moment of the political within Marxism."[25] Democracy thereby becomes, Critchley continues, "a manifestation of dissensus, a dissensus that disturbs the order by which government wishes to depoliticize society."[26] From this perspective, any search for radical democracy must embrace the pluralist nature of democracy as a process, which Mouffe calls agonistics, although that process, in contrast to Mouffe's notion of the political, can never be found in the state arena; democracy is the very process that disrupts the state of order. By that token, Miguel Abensour, in his Machiavellian reading of the political Marx, overtly contrasts democracy and the state. For Abensour, democracy "is not a political regime but primarily an action, a modality of political agency," whereas state power "is a menace to democracy or even tends toward its destruction."[27] This radical democratic line of thought, construing democracy as a subversive political process rather than a state of political conditions, is particularly articulated by political philosopher Jacques Rancière.

In his book *Hatred of Democracy*, Rancière detects two interconnected functions of democracy. The first aims to conjure a particular state of society, in opposition to governments built on dictatorship, tyranny, and totalitarianism. The subsequent function of democracy is to produce institutionalized practices to defend this societal state against relentless threats. Rancière focuses not on external threats to the democratic state but on an endemic threat that is embedded in democracy itself. For Rancière, the democratic state of society is under constant attack from what he calls *democratic life*: the disruptive collective practices that challenge governmental authority and the social division between governors and governed. Rancière discerns in democracy an embedded notion of "the power of the people, which is not the power of the population or of the majority, but the power of anyone at all."[28]

The democratic government is threatened, Rancière continues, by the disruptive aspects of democratic life. To tackle this subversive threat, the democratic government actively opposes "the double excess of political democratic life and mass individualism."[29] The defining social hierarchy of the democratic state—the division between governors and governed—is here motivated by notions of people as being apolitical and individualistic consumers in desperate need of political representation. Offstage political activities, that is, politics aside from the state arena, are not only understood as excessive but as a direct threat to governmental authority. Democratic government is, therefore, especially concerned with restraining this "double excess" of consumerist idleness and extraparliamentary democratic life. As Rancière puts it, "the 'government of anybody and everybody' is bound to attract the hatred of all those who are entitled to govern men by their birth, wealth, or science."[30] This power of "anyone at all" destabilizes the fundamental division between governors and governed by attacking the very heart of state authority. This is, Rancière concludes, an outright scandal for democratic government; the public-private distinction so essential for the democratic state is defied through the political nature of democratic life. In other words, the decisive challenging of the constitutive division between the governors and the people they seek to govern threatens the very foundation of the democratic state.

Jacques Rancière's radical democratic theory captures key dimensions of democratic conflict. Whereas Abensour recognizes a conflict between democracy and the state,[31] Rancière theorizes the conflictual nature of democracy itself. By depicting democratic life as a severe threat to the democratic state, Rancière encourages us not only to explore the political processes of radical democracy but also to dispose and study democracy's endemic conflict between the government and those it tries to govern. Rancière's radical democratic theorization exposes, as in the case of anti-police riots in Sweden, the very boundaries of any political project submitted to the logic of governance. In this regard, as we shall see, the Rancièrian scheme also finds some clear resonance with the scandalous tradition of anarchism, the political ideology that advocates nothing less than pure anarchy.

This book, then, springs from the theoretical dissensus of the radical democratic school. It builds on two empirical inquiries: a qualitative case study of intense democratic antagonism and a literature review of that antagonism construed within the anarchist tradition. Rancière's theorization informs the case study through an analysis of the collective experiences of the vivid democratic life in Husby and the confining responses of the democratic state. We will deepen this critical analysis by exploring a political ideology concerned precisely with that social conflict, the anarchist tradition that is generically adverse to every form of governance. This tandem inquiry accordingly employs two research methods. The Swedish case study draws on in-depth interviews conducted in relation to the Husby riots. The literature review of anarchism and democracy, which composes the main part of this book, links the social antagonism of the Swedish anti-police riots to the anarchist tradition by tracing the genealogy of democracy within anarchist thought. Building on these two empirical analyses, the book outlines a layered anarchist critique of democracy to elaborate what I call the Impossible Argument.

Anti-Police Riots
in Sweden

On a quiet Sunday night in May 2013, at a deserted parking lot in central Husby, multiple cars are set on fire. When the police arrive to investigate the arson, they are attacked. Retreating from a downpour of stones, the police call for immediate backup. When additional forces arrive, they too are confronted by unidentified stone-throwers. The attack sites appear to be strategically well-chosen. Police cars are repeatedly hit, and officers fail to incarcerate the vanishing aggressors. After a long night under attack, the police forecast an escalation of the civil unrest in Husby. The following night, in the blooming Swedish spring, five hundred armed police officers enter the small neighborhood, determined to restore social order. As the police scale up their operation, now including severe beatings of community residents, accompanied by overtly racist insults, people in Husby, themselves out on the streets to defend social order, are increasingly provoked. The conflict in Husby rapidly escalates but then fades out during the third night of confrontation, only to recur in other parts of Sweden. The contagious and unruly conflict, the government soon declared, marked a severe threat to democracy.

This account of these intense May nights in the Swedish spring of 2013 builds on official police accounts, media reports, and in-depth interviews, which constitute the empirical components of a collective research project that analyzed these events.[1] The study documented how those May nights of confrontational social uprisings, framed in the media as urban riots, led to the immediate call for an official debate in the Swedish Parliament concerning the structural problems that allegedly triggered the conflict.[2] All across the political spectrum, state governors agreed that the causal explanation was the socioeconomic problems concentrated in Husby, albeit (unsurprisingly) disagreeing on how to address these issues; elected politicians eagerly competed on how to address their self-defined social problems. At the same time, governmental officials were unanimously silent on one point: the police.

Yet one week before the riots, as reported in national media, a grim police shooting had taken place in Husby, with sixty-nine-year-old Lenine Relvas-Martins not only killed by the police but his death deliberately covered up. While the police officially claimed to have verified that Martins was transported to the hospital by ambulance, witnessing neighbors reported that he had, in fact, been carried out on a stretcher into a hearse, obviously having been killed by the police in his home. Husby residents swiftly organized demonstrations to expose and protest police violence. The national media reported that these anti-police demonstrations were nonviolent, though sharply critical. Community organizers in Husby also expected violent clashes with the police and the weekend before the riot barbecues and festivities were arranged to dampen the predicted confrontation. On Friday and Saturday, nothing happened; but on Sunday night, May 19, when few people were out on the streets, the police were attacked.

This chapter analyzes democratic conflict in a local historical context. Guided by Rancière's theoretical vocabulary, we will discern how Husby's *democratic life* has recurrently been suppressed by Sweden's *democratic state*. We will see how that social antagonism intensified in the so-called Husby riots, producing a supposed threat to democracy.

The inquiry into Husby's democratic conflict draws on a collective research intervention. During the weeks following the initial uprisings in Husby, a self-organized ad hoc team of eight researchers, myself included, began documenting emic explanations of this spectacular event. Our ambition was to gather stories and accounts from Husby as soon as possible, while interpretations were still more fluid and less delimited by established historiography.[3] The profound suspicion in Husby about sharing information and experiences with unknown people asking questions posed a methodological obstacle. During those dramatic days in May, national and international media had more or less invaded Husby, eagerly speculating about the intentions and forces that prompted the riots.[4] Our question-asking agenda was, of course, unfolding in tandem with parallel inquiries conducted by the police.

We, therefore, had to approach the Husby community carefully when introducing our project and searching for interview participants. We gradually gained some acceptance and eventually ended up with thirty in-depth interviews. To distinguish ourselves from the parallel police and media inquiries, we soon abandoned our initial ambition to identify and interview people who had attacked the police. More in concert with our research focus—emic explanations of what journalists called "the Husby riots"—we searched for interviewees who had been on-site when the confrontations unfolded. The interviewees included men and women aged sixteen to eighty-one who lived or worked in Husby.

The initial findings of our study were first published as a popular report and presented at a well-attended public meeting in Husby. Apparent at this gathering, as in our interview study, was the vast inaccuracy of official representations (by the media and government) of Husby residents. For its part, the Husby community encompassed numerous individual and organizational voices who articulated themselves on a variety of religious, political, and cultural axes. Acknowledging this heterogeneity, our ethnographic study, nonetheless, identified collectively accumulated experiences. The following chapter focuses on the experiences specifically linked to the theme of this book: the social antagonism between governors and the people they try to govern.

"We Would Never Call the Cops"

As we saw in the introductory chapter, radical democratic theory typically acknowledges the contentious, conflictual nature of democracy. In this vein Jacques Rancière offers a theoretical scheme in which democratic life—people's political activity outside the state arena—is recurrently targeted by the democratic state: the police-accompanied decision-makers of municipalities or nation-states. The Rancièrian notion of democratic conflict, the antagonism between governors and governed, finds notable resonance in the Husby case. The community residents whom our research team interviewed in relation to the 2013 Husby riots emphasized how local organizing and political initiatives have repeatedly been suppressed by, as one interviewee put it, "the people in power." Typifying this antagonism, Husby residents recalled the struggles around the state-instigated housing project called Järvalyftet [The Järva Vision]. The objective of Järvalyftet, as formulated by its architects at Stockholm City Hall, was to transform

Husby and the neighboring suburbs into "an attractive city district to which people want to move and settle down."[5] Interviewed residents in Husby, however, casually described Järvalyftet as something of a collaboration between state and capital, between the government and housing companies.

One interviewed Husby resident recalled how "they just approached us with a letter, stating that our houses would be rebuilt, with an updated standard and price, and that we had to move somewhere else."[6] The interviewee, a politically engaged Husby resident in his early eighties, overtly questioned the housing company's right to govern the residents' living situation. He further described how this defiance was backed up by massive protests against the upcoming evictions. Social mobilization against the housing project challenged, using Rancière's theoretical vocabulary, the entitlement to govern on the basis of wealth; the property owner Svenska Bostäder was given no legitimacy to dictate the residents' basic living situation. On a similar note, the joint knowledge production of municipal urban planners and commercial housing companies was also called into question. Interviewees described how Svenska Bostäder had arranged a so-called "residential dialogue," with people across the community actually taking the dialogue notion seriously and forwarding their opinions on Järvalyftet. The interviewed residents portrayed how they soon discovered that "dialogue" simply meant the announcement of ready-made decisions. Disregarding the critical viewpoints and suggested modifications produced by the genuine experts on Husby—the residents themselves—the housing project was eventually carried out precisely as planned by its original architects.

In Husby, Järvalyftet was accordingly understood as a poorly informed project. Therefore, the entitlement to govern, here on the basis of science, became increasingly illegitimate. From the Rancièrian perspective, the governors-governed hierarchy—the social division incarnated in Järvalyftet—was clearly challenged by the democratic life stirring in Husby. A notable example here is the overt resistance against the dislocation of Husby Civic Hall, described by interviewees as an important meeting point for the community, built and maintained by those using it. Interviewees described how politicians decided, without further ado, to displace and scale down the Civic Hall. When decision-makers continued to ignore the disapproving objections from Civic Hall users, a group of Husby residents chose to occupy the building to, as stated in their press release, "manifest enhanced self-determination."[7] The government responded to this surge of democratic life by scaling up its displacement plans, eventually imposing the decision despite the residents' distinct acts of defiance. Interviewed residents described this procedure as frustratingly familiar. They recalled how the Care Centre had been removed despite a petition with thousands of signatures, which in turn invoked collective memories of dismantled health and swimming centers, as well as the local library.

Nonetheless, our reading of the Husby riots should not be reduced to the frustrated collective experience of those denied access to governmental decision-making. As suggested by Paulina de los Reyes, the social conflict in Husby also exemplifies how the state of society can be actively challenged.[8] For instance, on the day after the initial attacks against the police, a local organization named Megafonen [The Megaphone] called a press conference in Husby to provide media and government actors with a locally rooted contextualization of the riots. Megafonen construed the events as inevitable due to frustrations caused by "blocked democratic channels": an open conflict, as they put it, "between the police and the residents of Husby."[9] Their swift initiative—broadcasting a locally rooted account before the usual acclaimed government, media, and academic experts—certainly forced journalists to search for narratives that complemented the typical criminalizing explanations.[10] The unusual press conference and its underlying organizational rigor generated scholarly interpretations of the Megafonen phenomenon as "the emergence of a new urban social movement" and "an autonomous, non-violent and organizationally embedded movement for social justice."[11]

Though the role of Megafonen should not be underestimated, it cannot be reduced to a simplistic and unanimous representation of Husby residents. People who live and work in Husby do, of course, express and construe their collective experiences in quite different ways. In spite of this obvious social fact, Megafonen was quickly assigned the function of representing Husby. The Swedish media soon reduced that representation into a binary position: either to encourage or to condemn the violence directed at the police. Megafonen insistently refused such a one-dimensional positioning, instead advancing their own analysis, before finally being disqualified as a useful representative for the mass media. De los Reyes argues that this insubordination defied the very preconditions for speaking in representative democracies,[12] in turn fueling the governmental imagery of riots in Husby as a threat to democracy itself.

This notion of *democratic threat* becomes quite conspicuous from a Rancièrian perspective. Interviewees expressed frustration over how their political activity—Husby's *democratic life*—was constantly bypassed by the government. One interviewee, with extensive non-European life experience, described Sweden as "a democratic country without democracy in everyday life."[13] On this note, interviewed Husby residents emphasized that vibrant democratic life was either ignored or suppressed by the government. In response to the government's "hatred of democracy," to use the language of Jacques Rancière, Husby residents have developed practices that foster mutual aid beyond the welfare offered by the state:

> In need of help, we would never call the cops. No, we call each other. And we don't have some leader if that's what you think. We're not some kind of gang. We're just people who are raised here, and we support each other. Society cannot be trusted, because we know how it works, so we'll have to do everything ourselves.[14]

The quoted interviewee, a Husby resident in his early forties, emphasizes how affinity characterizes local relations, regardless of state initiatives that provide alleged welfare and social security. As we have seen, his distrust in "society," here referring to majority rule in Sweden, stems from a collectively experienced inability to participate meaningfully in the procedures of governmental decision-making. Magnus Hörnqvist shows how this discontent was propelled by collective memories of a functioning Swedish welfare state, from which Husby residents are fiercely excluded.[15] Nonetheless, as underlined in the above excerpt, the people of Husby cannot afford to settle for mere discontent; instead, they organize themselves on their own terms to address political problems directly.

In the Rancièrian scheme, it is precisely these political activities of mutual aid and direct action—democratic life outside of the state arena—that, for the democratic state, are excessive and outright threatening. This conflict, in Rancière's radical democratic theorization, is a defining contour of democracy itself. In Husby, as we will see in the following section, the long-lived social conflict between those entitled to govern and those who defy such entitlement constitutes an imperative historical background to the intensified conflict of May 2013.

"The Fires Continued"

Husby's conflictual May nights were immediately conceptualized and broadcasted as "the Husby riots"; yet our interviewees, by contrast, use a variety of alternative wordings to avoid the pejorative stigma typically attached to riot terminology. With our Rancièrian analysis, however, we acknowledge that people with sufficient power to govern others most certainly understand riots as problematic. In his book *Riot. Strike. Riot*, Joshua Clover similarly postulates that "the riot, comprising practices arrayed against threats to social reproduction, cannot be anything but political." In the modern political realm, Clover concludes, "police and riot thus come to presuppose each other."[16] Yet across society, we should not forget, the scale of positions stretches from those that completely embrace the riot (most clearly, participants themselves), to those that willingly use their own or others' bodies to restrain it (most typically, the police). Everyone else who navigates these confrontational positions dwells somewhere in between.

In Sweden, in the spring of 2013, violent confrontations between the police and their attackers produced a variety of opinions, interpretations, and positions among the people who lived and worked in Husby. As other scholars have pointed out, the Husby events must be understood in the context of "rapidly increasing social inequalities, racialized territorial stigmatization and lack of democracy in urban-restructuring processes."[17] Accordingly, our interviewed residents, despite all their diversities, typically regarded social explanations as deeply rooted in the conflictual political experience accumulated in the local community. As one interviewee put it:

> The people who started this—this revolution, as we call it— are human beings. It's no coincidence that this is people that feels completely ignored, deprived of their voice and ability to participate.[18]

This contextualization, which connects the violent May confrontations to collective memories of deprived political influence, is recurrently elaborated by interviewed Husby residents. Furthermore, interviewees witnessing the confrontations firsthand offered explanations about the subsequent conflict escalation and the shockingly explicit state violence. As shown by Janne Flyghed and Kristina Boréus, interviewees recalled how the police, clearly haunted by their failure to handle the attack during the first night's upheaval, soon directed their violence against mere onlookers. Flyghed and Boréus document how the police combined dog attacks, baton beatings, and racist insults with a fierce disinclination to communicate with residents.[19] These shocking collective experiences were revisited to explain why, when cars began to burn the following night, people packed the streets of Husby:

> The fires continued. Many parents had no problem with this, believing that the police got what they deserved. On the first night, the police had the dogs attacking civilians. When the youngsters threw stones, and the parents stood between them and the police, they sent out the dogs. "Bite! Bite!" they shouted. "Fucking monkeys! Fucking niggers!" I heard many of these degrading insults. The police certainly pushed to worsen the situation the following day.[20]

The quoted interviewee portrays youth and parents as momentarily united and, thus, unanimously targeted by the police. State violence directed against nonviolent parents, obviously concerned with maintaining public safety, destabilized the distinction between observers and participants. In this particular situation, attacking and counterattacking the police appears to have emanated from a certain level of social legitimacy. Our interviews indicate that the attack on the police was silently approved by people on the street, at least to some extent. Such legitimacy was quite noticeable in an interview with a police-friendly Husby resident, clearly frustrated with people that "just stood there and watched, not stopping them nor telling them to drop the stones and walk away."[21] Nonetheless, that social legitimacy was indeed restricted, carefully confined by distinct temporal and spatial boundaries.

Silent approval for the attack on the police, albeit fragile and recognized only momentarily, must be understood, I believe, in the light of Husby's democratic life, which is constantly suppressed by the democratic state of Sweden. As documented by Alejandro Gonzalez, when armed police aggressively entered Husby, people experienced it as an invasion of their public space.[22] The invasive state violence thereby embodied the collectively accumulated experiences of repressed democratic life; the moment of violent confrontation between stone-throwers and the police intensified the social antagonism so vividly remembered in Husby. When such a conflict intensifies, so does the search for functional political tactics. One resistance tactic in particular was recalled from the local historical repertoire:

> We, some youth, went to the office of Svenska Bostäder. We threw stones, we attacked their entire office with stones, and that was only directed at them, nothing else, no people were targeted, because this was about discontent. That was on a Friday. On Monday, they call me and said, "We are ready to discuss with you. What do you want?"[23]

This interview excerpt illustrates how stone-throwing was already part of the resistance repertoire in Husby (as in so many places around the globe). The interviewee here explains how precision is key for this particular tactic, which indicates how stone-throwing is also carefully conditioned. According to the interviewee, the attack on Svenska Bostäder addressing the housing company's severe reduction in youth employment was deliberately executed without harm to human beings or neighboring facilities. When this tactic was reactivated in May 2013, targeted property destruction once again became instrumental. In the following interview excerpt, I (ML) have just asked a twenty-year-old Husby resident (R) why he thinks cars were targeted:

> **R:** What else is there to burn? Houses? Apartments? No, people live there. That would be going too far. Cars were torched to entice the police. When the police didn't come, people continued torching cars until they did. The purpose was to get to the police, not to burn some guy's car, a neighbor's car. Burning cars wasn't the purpose, but it had to be done.
> **ML:** What do you mean by "get to the police"?
> **R:** They entrapped the police to deal with them in their own way.
> **ML:** With stones?
> **R:** Yes, by throwing stones.[24]

The quoted interviewee patiently explains how people only burned cars so they could target the police. By enticing the police to specific sites, the attackers had an important strategic advantage: police cars could be efficiently attacked from the above footbridges that allowed safe escape routes. For the interviewee, the destruction of cars was an entirely instrumental enterprise, unfortunate for individual car owners but relatively safe compared to alternative police baits.

Yet it was precisely these car burnings that drained the social legitimacy of the attack. As one interviewee put it, anti-police fury should target "the police station, not people's cars."[25] The burning of cars in Husby was, therefore, generally disliked among the interviewed residents. Direct violence against the police, however, was much more delicately discussed. Some interviewees described the attacks as a way to "speak up" and "protest" against a political system that disables meaningful participation. Others emphasized that violent attacks against the police are, in fact, counterproductive. What the interviewees nonetheless were careful to highlight was that the violent confrontation between the police and the Husby residents must be understood in its local historical context.

The experiences from Husby make clear that democratic life, using Rancière's theoretical vocabulary, had long been suppressed; the hatred of democracy has been enduring. The conflict embedded in democracy—between governors and those they try to govern—has a remembered history in Husby. Subsequently, when the government's police force invaded the neighborhood, in May 2013, the burning conflict intensified. Even though most residents did not partake in violence against the police, the historical antagonism seems to have informed a significant legitimacy, albeit conditioned and fragile, for these attacks. During the third night of intensified conflict in Husby, this legitimacy rapidly dissolved. Our interviewees reported that parents had had enough, and youngsters were increasingly criticized for their actions at home. After two nights of violent confrontation increasingly drained of social legitimacy, people started to intervene more actively to restrain the stone-throwers:

> I see riot police on one side. On the other, I see maybe eight, ten elderly women, some with veils and others without, Chileans, Swedes, Moroccans, and Tunisians. They form a human chain, standing there crying. They don't want the cops to get hurt. Although the cops deserve it—they are pigs—that was it for me. These youngsters were so close to hitting [the people in the

human chain], although they were shouting at them to get out of the way. When I saw these people there crying, I run over to shout, "That's enough! Walk away! People's moms could get stoned."[26]

This interview excerpt illustrates the draining of legitimacy for violent confrontation. The symbolism of "people's moms" getting hurt obviously called for a tactical retreat. Alejandro Gonzalez argues that such family imagery, typically used by Husby residents in reference to their community, reinforces a sense of intimacy and mutual responsibility.[27] Even though "the cops deserve" additional attacks, the interviewee quoted above comes to evaluate confrontations as too dangerous, with community members being put at severe risk. On a similar note, other interviewees described how people grew increasingly concerned about conflict escalation, with non-Husby residents beginning to participate in the uprising. Although understanding that people came "to get back at the police," as one interviewee put it, the residents of Husby seem to have been quite unsure about these nonlocals' ability to read community legitimacy signals. When rumors began to spread about outsiders arriving to join the struggle against the police, this seemed to jeopardize local control over the situation. To preserve democratic life in Husby, the intensified conflict with the democratic state had to be restrained.

From the government's perspective, however, *the police* eventually restored social order in Husby; after a few nights of strong police presence, people stopped burning cars and throwing stones. Associated parliamentary discussions soon returned to the usual theme of how to aid poor urban areas. Yet what had happened in Husby also denoted, as government representatives so keenly pointed out, a severe threat. Our Rancièrian reading, I would argue, actually validates that threat: defiance of the governors-governed division taunts the very foundation of democracy itself.

"Threat to Democracy"

I think the dividing line stretches right across Husby: between people who desire peace, who want to stop perpetrators, have their property respected, and move freely in their own neighborhood, and the few violators who actually believe in the workings of violence.[28]

In a peculiar way, the above statement from Sweden's prime minister apparently corresponds to the Husby experience. Although most certainly portraying a division among Husby residents, Prime Minister Fredrik Reinfeldt inadvertently reflected the Rancièrian distinction between democratic life and the democratic state. Husby residents surely struggle for "peace," "respect," and "to move freely in their own neighborhood." The residents' counterpart consists of people who "believe in the workings of violence" so strongly that it has become their profession. This dividing line between police and people in Husby represents a clear recollection of social antagonism. In May 2013, that conflict intensified into fierce confrontation. The state responded accordingly, rapidly mobilizing state violence on a massive scale to, as the police officially put it, restrain the "severe threat to democracy."[29]

For politically engaged Husby residents, the official discourse about defending democracy was a downright insult. Interviewees starkly renounced explanations about riots deriving from some indifferent, uneasy youth culture,[30] while government officials insisted on blaming restive and adrenaline-seeking youngsters for triggering the riot. Marcus Lauri shows how politicians called for enhanced disciplinary measures to address such disturbing social elements. The mandate of the police, politicians argued in the wake of violent confrontations, had to be accompanied by programs that took youngsters off the streets and placed them in employment or education. The *soft policing* of Husby was, Lauri continues, to be enacted in concert with what government officials referred to as "the good forces": parents, social workers, imams, priests, and civil society overall.[31] "The Husby riots" were accordingly construed as apolitical expressions of an individual, consumerist youth culture, which requires disciplinary activities like school or work to avoid social unrest. At the same time, the riots were also portrayed as political violence to motivate and legitimate massive police intervention. In defense of democracy, the government swiftly aimed to suppress what Rancière calls "the double excess of political democratic life and mass individualism."[32]

The interviewees depicted the massive police invasion as yet another attack on Husby's vibrant political activity, ignored or suppressed by municipal and state governors. Invasive police forces merely embodied that collective experience; the state's violent response answered to the very foundation of democracy, the division between governors and governed. Political activity outside of the state arena, what Rancière calls democratic life, threatened the legitimacy of the democratic state. Democratic life posed a democratic threat, and governors responded accordingly.

The Husby case illustrates how governmental defense of democracy can translate into arrogant disqualification of people's political activities, accompanied by violent repression. The confrontations between police and stone-throwers in May 2013 continued the fires of an ongoing democratic conflict in Husby. The attack against the police was understood, though decidedly problematized, as temporarily challenging the hierarchical division between police and people, governors and governed. Experiences of suppressed political activity thereby fueled the bounded legitimacy of what official voices so keenly labeled "the Husby riots." The violent confrontation with the police was, in fact, constrained specifically by Husby's democratic life. Drained of legitimacy, stone-throwing quickly became a non-functional resistance tactic; within a few days, attacks against the police had completely died out. It was, in other words, the people—and not the police—who initiated, restrained, and ended the intensified conflict.

The Husby residents did not speak of victory. One interviewee poetically declared that "cars are burning, yet problems persist."[33] The aggregate experience of political activity in Husby articulated a lack of meaningful political influence and collective self-determination:

> We definitely don't decide for ourselves. It's always been like this. Democracy allows us to put a ballot in a box every fourth year, but in reality we don't decide anything at all. We don't make decisions; we vote for others to decide on our behalf. That is our beautiful democracy.[34]

Here, the quoted interviewee, a social worker and Husby resident in his early twenties, portrays democracy as deeply problematic. Democracy, he reasons cynically, is not people deciding for themselves; it is people deprived of that very power. This critical analysis finds some clear resonance in Rancièrian radical democratic theory; it exposes democracy's endemic conflict between governors and governed. It carries a profound critique of the state of democracy. The following chapter deepens this critique of democracy's governors-governed antagonism by venturing into the history of anarchism.

Anarchism and Democracy

To be *governed* is to be kept in sight, inspected, spied upon, directed, law-driven, numbered, enrolled, indoctrinated, preached at, controlled, estimated, valued, censured, commanded, by creatures who have neither the right, nor the wisdom, nor the virtue to do so.

To be *governed* is to be at every operation, at every transaction, noted, registered, enrolled, taxed, stamped, measured, numbered, assessed, licensed, authorized, admonished, forbidden, reformed, corrected, punished.

It is, under the pretext of public utility, and in the name of the general interest, to be placed under contribution, trained, ransomed, exploited, monopolized, extorted, squeezed, mystified, robbed; then, at the slightest resistance, the first word of complaint, to be repressed, fined, despised, harassed, tracked, abused, clubbed, disarmed, choked, imprisoned, judged, condemned, shot, deported, sacrificed, sold, betrayed; and, to crown all, mocked, ridiculed, outraged, dishonored.

That is government; that is its justice; that is its morality.[1]

The above portrait, depicting the experiential meaning of being governed, is formulated in one of the first pioneering publications of the anarchist tradition. The epilogue of Pierre-Joseph Proudhon's *General Idea of the Revolution in the Nineteenth Century*—produced in the aftermath of the 1848 revolutions—elaborates a stark aversion for every manifestation of governance; it sets the antiauthoritarian tone of the anarchist tradition. In parallel with that defiance, anarchism also nurtures a desire, a hope—a political struggle—for being ungovernable.

"You poor judges, poor slaves of the government," wrote imprisoned anarchist Kanno Sugako, having been charged with high treason for plotting against the Japanese emperor. On the eve of her execution in January 1911, Kanno voiced distinct anarchist defiance of governance, entailed by the notion of being ungovernable: "I should be angry at you, but I pity you instead. Here I am bound by this barred window, but my thoughts still spread their wings in the free world of ideas. Nothing can bind my thoughts or interfere with them. You may live for a hundred years, but what is a life without freedom, a life of slavery, worth?"[2]

In this chapter, we will deepen our analysis of the governors-governed antagonism—recognized through the Husby case as a catalyst for democratic conflict—by outlining its elaboration in the anarchist tradition. Our journey through the history of anarchist thought traces critical approaches to democracy in relation to anarchy. We will see how the anarchist tradition nurtures an emblematic defiance of governance, while the relationship between democracy and anarchy is notably diverse. We will explore these variances and changes over time: the classical *anarchist critique* of democracy, the post-classical *anarchist reclamation* of democracy, and the *reclaimed critique* in contemporary anarchism. Our study of democracy's genealogy within the history of anarchist thought will travel back and forth through the anarchist chronology, here recognized as classical anarchism (1840–1939) and post-classical anarchism (1940–), to trace the tradition's multifaceted understandings of democracy.

In being what Spanish anarchist Federica Montseny called "an ideal without boundaries,"[3] the amorphous contours of *anarchism*, the political ideology advocating *anarchy*, allow for a broad variety of ideological strands. The anarchist tradition accordingly targets compound strains of domination: economic, political, and social. As formulated by one of England's most prominent anarchist organizers in the late nineteenth century, Charlotte Wilson, anarchism means a struggle against the tendency to dominate:

> The leading manifestations of this obstructive tendency at this present moment are Property, or domination over things, the denial of the claim of others to their use; and Authority, the government of man by man, embodied in majority rule; that theory of representation which, whilst admitting the claim of the

individual to self-guidance, renders him the slave of the simulacrum that now stands for society.[4]

A key effort of anarchist thought is, thus, to extend the socialist critique of capitalist property relations; anarchism detests, as the above excerpt from Charlotte Wilson underlines, the very idea of authority, the instrument of government. Anarchism is, therefore, as Voltairine de Cleyre once put it, a "belief that all forms of external authority must disappear to be replaced by self-control only."[5] In quite a similar vein, Emma Goldman defined anarchy as "the negation of all forms of authority,"[6] encompassing "freedom from government of every kind."[7] In the early 1900s, Emma Goldman became a well-known proponent of anarchism in North America. In the aftermath of the 1901 assassination of President McKinley, Goldman was accused by the authorities to have incited the self-defined anarchist assassin. She was soon referred to as an Anarchist Queen, famously labeled the most dangerous woman in America.[8] To the governments of her time, Goldman—and the anarchist movement she was involved in—represented a serious threat.[9]

Emma Goldman was, like Voltairine de Cleyre and other influential anarchists of this generation, radicalized in the aftermath of the Haymarket tragedy.[10] In Chicago, in early May 1886, a demonstration in support of the eight-hour workday ended with violent clashes between police and workers. Eight anarchists were eventually charged for the police deaths caused by the clash, and four were later hanged.[11] The anarchist movement was now injected with renewed energy. In what political scientist Kathy Ferguson calls "the Haymarket effect,"[12] this historical event sparked the anarchist tradition; it fueled the critique of governance and prompted struggles to become ungovernable. In this chapter, we will deepen our critical analysis of the governors-governed conflict by exploring the various approaches to democracy produced within the unfolding history of anarchist thought.

It should be noted that the ideological tradition of anarchism is, as historian Maia Ramnath points out, "one contextually specific manifestation among a larger—indeed global—tradition of antiauthoritarian, egalitarian thought/praxis."[13] Considering that, anarchism should certainly not be understood as the only ideological tradition in which we may look for an antiauthoritarian critique of democracy; it is, nonetheless, a living tradition that remains considerably consistent, widespread, and textually resourceful.[14] At its very starting point as a social movement in the 1870s, anarchism was a thoroughly global movement. Political scientist Benedict Anderson suggests that "following the collapse of the First International and Marx's death in 1883, anarchism, in its characteristically variegated forms, was the dominant element in the self-consciously internationalist left."[15] On a similar note, Ferguson observes that anarchist journals frequently reported affiliated struggles in Africa, South America, and Asia.[16] Given the transnational character of the anarchist movement, this ideological tradition has fostered plural and divergent evaluations of and responses to the democratic state. Due to the extensive written body of work produced by anarchists over the years, we have good reason to explore the anarchist tradition to study the social antagonisms of democracy.

A literature review of an ideological *tradition*, and not merely of a sole thinker, immediately raises questions about how to uncover, weigh, and categorize the textual canon. The initial method is obviously to include the most recurrent cross references: text and statements canonized by anarchist writers themselves. The key texts of the anarchist tradition have successively been identified by scholars like Paul Eltzbacher, Max Nettlau, George Woodcock, Peter Marshall, and Ruth Kinna.[17] The literature review presented in this chapter outlines how key anarchist thinkers have understood and approached democracy. However, and this I find methodologically imperative, we must guard against uncritical reproduction of some static textual canon; anarchism, like any ideological tradition, is constantly revised by those who draw upon its sources.[18] Emma Goldman, for instance, actively sought to link individualist thinkers to her political theory, just as anarchists in the late 1960s revitalized Goldman's thought, all of which contributed to the continuous modification of the canonizing process.[19] Contemporary anarchists now tend to view Goldman as one of the movement's key figures.[20] This assertion has in turn enlightened the account of female participation in the anarchist movement. Ferguson documents the fact that although most canonized texts were written by male anarchists, "the anarchist groups during Goldman's time and place were roughly one-third or even one-half women."[21]

In other words, lack of written sources unfortunately forces our reading to encompass a disproportionate ratio of women's contributions to the anarchist tradition. Analytical focus on internally important texts thereby carries the risk of excluding important anarchist thinkers, thus, reproducing a male-dominated anarchist canon.[22] The following literature review, while incorporating the typical canonized anarchist texts, also aims to dispose oft-forgotten contributions from female anarchist thinkers. Furthermore, this reading of original anarchist texts will be complemented by scholarly analyses, commentary, and contextualization emanating from the research field of anarchist studies.[23] These scholarly texts are not, I would argue, easily distinguishable from original anarchist writings; researchers in this field often tend to situate their contributions in the anarchist tradition. Our study of democracy and anarchy, then, weaves together key anarchist texts (from the early nineteenth century onward) with affiliated scholarly research on the anarchist tradition. The selection of texts is primarily guided by the drive of this book to further the radical democratic theorization of the division between governors and governed, the chief social antagonism targeted by the anarchist tradition.

With this analytical focus, I believe that Emma Goldman's theorization, along with Errico Malatesta's unblemished critique of democracy, which I will introduce in the following section, provide especially fruitful entry points for our examination of the anarchist tradition. As we will see, Malatesta and Goldman inventively combined the individualist and communist strands of classical anarchism. They also cultivated well-established links to key thinkers across the anarchist movement; Malatesta had a tremendous network through his work with the First International;[24] Goldman had a wide editorial influence that also extended into post-classical anarchism.[25] Since Malatesta and Goldman were both dynamic political thinkers, reflecting on the various political struggles they participated in, their writings are particularly useful for apprehending an anarchist critique of the democratic state. Hence, we will deepen our study of democracy's social antagonism through the profound anarchist critique of *governance*, the "violence, coercion, forcible imposition of the will of the governors upon the governed," as Malatesta so tellingly put it in the late 1800s.[26]

The first part of this chapter introduces the *anarchist critique* of democracy, a defiant composition arrayed against governmental authority, representation, and majority rule. As we will see, this compound critique soon translates into a reinterpretation, a radicalization—an *anarchist reclamation*—of the democracy concept. The second part of this chapter outlines the notions of direct participatory democracy, made equivalent to or perceived as a step toward anarchy. In parallel with these inclinations to radicalize and (re)claim democracy—ideas that still linger in contemporary anarchist thought—a divergent tendency has developed, again dissociating democracy from anarchy. The third part of this chapter explores this *reclaimed critique* in relation to non-human life and, finally, to radical democracy.

Anarchist Critique

> We are neither for a majority nor for a minority government, neither for democracy not for dictatorship. We are for the abolition of the *gendarme*. We are for the freedom of all and for free agreement, which will be there for all when no one has the means to force others, and all are involved in the good running of society. We are for anarchy.[27]

When Malatesta's polemical article "Neither Democrats, nor Dictators: Anarchists" was published in May 1926, Italy had turned into a full-fledged fascist regime under the leadership of Benito Mussolini. Precisely in this political environment, Errico Malatesta chose to attack not only dictatorship, which would be the obvious adversary in this context, but also democracy. He demanded total abolition of the gendarme, the state's police and military forces.[28] In opposition to democracy, Malatesta called for anarchy. His motivation was simply the fact that "where there is government, namely authority, that authority resides in the majority."[29] As we will see, Malatesta extracted his categorical rejection of democracy from a compound *anarchist critique* of governance deeply rooted in the tradition's denunciation of authority, representation, and majority rule. Our ensuing examination of the governors-governed antagonism thus begins with the classical anarchist struggle against authority.

Against Authority

In the influential pamphlet *Anarchy*, written in 1891, Errico Malatesta located the anarchist struggle in opposition to "the very principle of government, the principle of authority."[30] By this token, critique of authority legitimates and transcends the anarchist defiance of government, in turn propelling a struggle against various forms of oppression.

"The authority that prevails in government," stated the classical anarchist Élisée Reclus, "corresponds to that which holds sway in families."[31] The same antipathy for authority had already been formulated by Proudhon (as we saw in the opening quote of this chapter),[32] which set the characteristic antiauthoritarian tone of anarchism. Proudhon was also responsible for the movement's self-identification with the term "anarchy," then as now commonly associated with violent chaos. In a famous passage from his magnum opus *What Is Property*, first published in 1840, Proudhon consecutively denounced every form of state government. "Well you are a democrat?" he lets the reader ask him. "No," Proudhon replies, "I am an anarchist."[33] Owing much to this passage, the antiauthoritarian socialism of the late nineteenth century was soon articulated more precisely as *anarchism*, a political movement advocating, as Proudhon put it, "Anarchy, the absence of a master, of a sovereign, such is the form of government to which we are every day approximating."[34]

The ensuing formation of the anarchist *movement* and its ideological tradition is also primarily indebted to the iconic, larger-than-life revolutionary Mikhail Bakunin. Stemming from a radical reading of Hegel, Bakunin polemically declared that the state "is the most flagrant, the most cynical, and the most complete negation of humanity."[35] On this note, in "The Illusion of Universal Suffrage," Bakunin conveys how social antagonism inevitably derives from governance:

> The instincts of the rulers, whether they legislate or execute the laws, are—by the very fact of their exceptional position—diametrically opposite. However democratic may be their feelings and their intentions, once they achieve the elevation of office they can only view society in the same way as a schoolmaster views his pupils, and between pupils and masters equality cannot exist....Whoever talks of political power talks of domination; but where domination exists there is inevitably a somewhat large section of society that is dominated, and those who are dominated quite naturally detest their dominators, while the dominators have no choice but to subdue and oppress those they dominate.[36]

From this Bakunist notion of government-caused social antagonism, which clearly resembles our governors-governed conflict, stems the anarchist struggle against parallel and interlinked forms of domination: the struggle against authority. Malatesta, for one, extracted from Bakunin a "radical criticism of the principle of authority and the State which embodies it; living [in Bakunin] is always the struggle against the two lies, the two guises, in which the masses are oppressed and exploited: democratic and dictatorial."[37] For Malatesta, government becomes "the consequence of the spirit of domination and violence with which some men have imposed themselves on others."[38] It is the "spirit of domination," as Charlotte Wilson also put it, which has incited anarchists to "declare war against its present principal forms of expression—property, and law manufactured and administered by majority rule."[39] Wilson announced that "this battle is for freedom, for the deliverance of the spirit of each one of us, and of humanity as a whole, from the government of man by man."[40] In classical anarchism, then, governance is typically codified as a particular structure—conspicuously embodied in the state—and a relationally situated principle of domination, called authority.

To identify an anarchist critique of democracy, especially regarding its direct participatory expressions, we must understand the tradition's enduring struggle against authority; anarchism characteristically targets authority's supreme concentration in governments, especially in our modern nation-states. It is against this backdrop that, in the second half of the nineteenth century, anarchism was articulated as a political movement. Along the lines of Proudhon, anarchists shared with socialists the critical analysis of power asymmetries produced by capitalism, but with an equally important addition: the social hierarchies sustained by institutions such as the Church and, not least, the state. Returning to Bakunin, we recognize the state as nothing less than "the ritual sacrifice of each individual and of every local association, an abstraction which destroys living society. It is the limitation, or rather the complete negation, of the so-called good of everyone."[41] In "Statism and Anarchy," Bakunin developed—in opposition to Karl Marx and Friedrich Engels—his critical evaluation of state power into a compound critique of government:

> Every state power, every government, by its very nature places itself outside and over the people and inevitably subordinates them to an organization and to aims which are foreign to and opposed to the real needs and aspirations of the people. We

declare ourselves the enemies of every government and every state power, and of governmental organization in general....No state, however democratic—not even the reddest republic—can ever give the people what they really want, i.e., the free self-organization and administration of their own affairs from the bottom upward, without any interference or violence from above.[42]

Bakunin's uncompromising approach toward state power—democratic states included—was fueled by a critique of authority, the social foundation for the governors-governed division. His conclusion was that every form of government must be abolished. Élisée Reclus, who, along with Bakunin, was one of the most prominent figures in the early anarchist movement, argued on an ensuing note that revolutionaries often fail to "imagine a free society operating without a conventional government, and as soon as they have overthrown their hated masters, they hasten to replace them with new ones."[43] Hence, the adamant critique of government so characteristic for classical anarchism seems to have allowed no pardon for the democratic state. Proudhon declared that even "with the most perfect democracy, we cannot be free."[44] For Proudhon the political goal was "neither monarchy, nor aristocracy, nor even democracy itself....No authority, no government, not even popular, that is the Revolution."[45] Another seventy years into the anarchist tradition, Italian anarchist Luigi Fabbri wrote in a similar vein in the essay "Fascism: The Preventive Counter-Revolution," critically reflecting on the democratic state in 1920s Italy:

> Democracy has been chasing its shadow for over a hundred years and devised all sorts of shapes for it; but, no matter what the form, the state has remained the champion of the interests of one class against another, the supporter and ally of the ruling class against the oppressed classes. Fascism in Italy has been an obvious instance of this, laying the democratic view of the state to rest once and for all.[46]

We recognize that the anarchist critique of authority may translate into a variety of political struggles that target the ever-occurring social divide between governors and governed. Although, in this vein, classical anarchism typically denounced democracy, construed in its representative guise, a few exceptions stand out. A prompt endeavor to appropriate democracy that played out in the early 1870s was the International Alliance of Socialist Democracy, a short-lived faction of the First International in which both Élisée Reclus and Mikhail Bakunin were central figures.[47] Here, the term "socialist democracy" presumably drew on Bakunin's previous call for a "social and democratic revolution."[48] Based on these writings, one could certainly read Bakunin's anarchism as democratic.[49] However, this temporary appropriation of the term democracy was most likely polemical, contrasted with what Bakunin understood to be a Marxian notion of democracy. Historian Robert Graham argues that following the First International debacle Bakunin abandoned his advocacy of association-based direct democracy to embrace an overall critique of binding policies.[50] Bakunin clearly expressed profound disbelief in the alleged Marxian notion of democracy, arguably established "through the dictatorship of a very strong and, so to say, despotic provisional government, that is, by the negation of liberty."[51] Hence, Bakunin's severe critique of governmental manifestations in whatever form would never allow a full-fledged democratic state; as we shall see, Bakunin argued that states not only maintain but also produce undesirable class structures. Consequently, Bakunin declared that the people's state can "signify only one thing: the destruction of the state."[52]

However, in parallel with the uncompromising critique of democracy, classical anarchism also cultivated an understanding of democracy in terms of a trajectory toward anarchy. We will later see how this notion flourished in post-classical anarchism, though sprouting from classical anarchist thought. Most notably, Proudhon explicitly advocated an anarchist project, through which "the principle of authority is forced to retire: it retires step by step, by a series of concessions, each one more insufficient than the other, of which the last, pure democracy, or direct government, ends in the impossible and the absurd."[53] When "we arrive at this last term, direct government," Proudhon continued, "there will be nothing for it but one of these two things, either to continue the development of government, or to proceed to the abolition of it."[54] This understanding of democracy as part of a trajectory was further developed by Alexander Berkman, Emma Goldman's inseparable companion.[55] The democratic state was for Berkman associated with majority rule, upheld by the principle of authority; it became a salient target for anarchist critique:

The essence of authority is invasion, the imposition of a superior will—generally superior only in point of physical force. The
menace of man-made authority is not in its potential abuse. That
may be guarded against. The fundamental evil of authority is its
use. The more paternal its character or the more humanistic its
symbols and mottoes, the greater its danger.... The democratic
authority of majority rule is the last pillar of tyranny. The last,
but the strongest.[56]

Here Berkman states that democracy is not desirable; it is the very
last stronghold of authority, yet an important step on the route toward
anarchy. This idea resembles Bakunin's uncompromising rejection of
"all legislation, all authority, and all privileged, licensed, official and legal
powers over us, even though arising from universal suffrage."[57] On this
note, when it comes to *representative* democracy, the anarchist tradition
is, in fact, unanimously critical.

Against Representation

The anarchist critique of representation in government and other forms
of rule clearly resembles that of the proto-anarchist philosopher William
Godwin,[58] typically considered by historians to be "the first to give a
clear statement of anarchist principles,"[59] and, therefore, he is regarded
as "the head of the tradition."[60] Godwin's "Enquiry Concerning Political
Justice," written at the very peak of the European Enlightenment in
the late eighteenth century, rejected the idea "that a majority should
overbear a minority.... This evil, inseparable from political government," Godwin argued, "is aggravated by representation, which removes
the powers of making regulations one step further from the people
whose lot it is to obey them." Godwin concluded that submission to
casting votes for elected representatives reduces the very vibrancy of
politics; "debate and discussion are, in their own nature, highly condu-
cive to intellectual improvement; but they lose this salutary character
the moment they are subjected to this unfortunate condition."[61] Even
though, as pointed out by historian George Woodcock, Godwin recognized the "merits of democracy over other political systems,"[62] he did
set a clear tone for the anarchist critique of representative government.

As anarchism became articulated as a political movement, the
critique of representative government—typically construed as

democracy—formed a keystone in its thought. Charlotte Wilson argued that "political methods in a democracy mean the art of obtaining command over the strength of numbers."[63] This critique of representative government was particularly developed by the late Bakunin. "If there is a State," Bakunin argued in "Statism and Anarchy," "there must be domination of one class by another.... The question arises, if the proletariat is to be the ruling class, over whom is it to rule?" In answer to his polemical question, Bakunin declared that this ruling class will "no longer represent the people, but only themselves and their claims to rulership over the people."[64] This critical forecast—that the state would maintain and produce class structures—entails a thorough critique of universal suffrage and the election of governmental representatives, which Bakunin understood as a key pillar of democracy:

> It was generally expected that once universal suffrage was established, the political liberty of the people would be assured. This turned out to be a great illusion.... The whole system of representative government is an immense fraud resting on this fiction: that the executive and legislative bodies elected by universal suffrage of the people must or even can possibly represent the will of the people.... Irrespective of their democratic sentiments or intentions, the rulers by virtue of their elevated position look down upon society as a sovereign regarding his subjects.... Political power means domination. And where there is domination, there must be a substantial part of the population who remain subjected to the domination of their rulers.[65]

Errico Malatesta, who often paid tribute to Bakunin's thought, picked up this notion of a new ruling class and stated that "government, parliamentary government included, is not merely powerless to resolve the social question and reconcile and satisfy everybody's interests, but of itself represents a privileged class with ideas, passions and interest."[66] Pyotr Kropotkin, a key figure in classical anarchism, similarly declared that "the State organization, having been the force to which the minorities resorted for establishing and organizing their power over the masses, cannot be the force which will serve to destroy these privileges."[67] The anarchist critique of political representation, understood as a central mechanism in the democratic state, was also pointedly rejected by Bakunin's friend and collaborator Carlo Cafiero:[68]

No intermediaries, no representatives who always end up representing no one but themselves, no one to moderate equality, no
more moderators of liberty, no new government, no new State,
even should it style itself popular or democratic, revolutionary
or provisional.[69]

In classical anarchism, then, critique of representation—and of
representative democracy—was intertwined with the question of
universal suffrage, the right to vote. This critique was deepened in the
early 1900s as anarchist women expressed critical views on supposed
emancipatory outcomes of universal suffrage.

In line with Lucy Parsons's declaration that "of all the modern
delusions, the ballot has certainly been the greatest,"[70] Chinese anarchist He-Yin Zhen argued that the "electoral system simply increases
[women's] oppression by introducing a third ruling group: Elite Women.
Even if oppression remains the same, the majority of women are still
taken advantage of by the minority of women."[71] In Zhen's feminist-leaning anarchism, which was a powerful strand within Chinese
anarchism at the time,[72] we recognize yet another layer in our search
for an anarchist critique of democracy: the renouncement of majority
rule. It is telling that Malatesta, our most articulate critic of democracy, so clearly spoke out against "majority rule," the arrangement that
"implies a minority that must either rebel or submit to the will of others."
Malatesta held that the rule of the many is only marginally better than
the rule of the few, contending that "those who really want 'government
of the people' in the sense that each can assert his or her own will, ideas
and needs, must ensure that no-one, majority or minority, can rule
over others; in other words, they must abolish government, meaning
any coercive organization, and replace it with the free organization of
those with common interests and aims."[73] On this note, the following
pages convey the pressing anarchist critique of majority rule—and the
democratic state—through its advancement in the political writings
of Emma Goldman.

Against Majority Rule

In her fierce critique of majority rule, Emma Goldman activated not
only a pioneering feminist analysis, as I elaborate elsewhere;[74] she
also drew upon the individualist strand of anarchist thought. Writing

amid feminism with a notorious focus on women's suffrage, Goldman rejected feminism as bourgeois, at best reformist. The feminists, Goldman contended, "foolishly believe that having a man's job, or professions, makes them free."[75] Commenting on Goldman's intense quarrel with the feminists of her time, Vivian Gornick, in her Goldman biography, simply declares that "Emma Goldman was not a feminist."[76] Goldman's rejection of feminism is quite characteristic for anarchist women, including Voltairine de Cleyre,[77] Leda Rafanelli,[78] and the revolutionaries of 1930s Spain.[79] Federica Montseny, a key theorist within this latter faction, polemically declared that "to propagate feminism is to foment masculinism; it is to create an immoral and absurd struggle between the sexes.... Feminism? Never! Humanism? Always!"[80]

It is in this vein that Goldman cultivated her disbelief in democratic elections. "Our modern fetish is universal suffrage," Goldman wrote in her essay "Women Suffrage," a fetish concealing "what people of intellect perceived fifty years ago: that suffrage is an evil, that it has only helped to enslave people, that it has but closed their eyes that they may not see how craftily they were made to submit."[81] Goldman's critique here resembles, possibly even refers to, Bakunin's evaluation of suffrage as an illusory, viscous route to freedom. Yet Goldman also went beyond Bakunin's analysis, cynically detesting the emancipatory potentials for female vote-casting:

> I see neither physical, psychological, nor mental reasons why women should not have the equal right to vote with men. But that cannot possibly blind me to the absurd notion that woman will accomplish that wherein man has failed. If she would not make things worse, she certainly could not make them better. [She] can give suffrage or the ballot no new quality, nor can she receive anything from it that will enhance her own quality. Her development, her freedom, her independence, must come from and through herself.[82]

Goldman refrained from essentialist notions of alleged female superiority, ideas about women being somehow better rulers than men. By that same token, Federica Montseny declared that "it is authority and domination that produce the evils in men in government and it will do the same to women. The answer to a better society is not female rulers, but a new society."[83] This idea was pointedly summarized by

Lucy Parsons: "the principle of rulership is in itself wrong; no man has any right to rule another."[84]

Precisely in the political context of popular demands for women's suffrage, feminist-leaning anarchists, especially Emma Goldman, took the opportunity to synthesize and propagate an anarchist contribution to feminist theory. Moreover, in this same proliferation, Goldman also incorporated, in her outspoken disbelief in suffrage as a means of emancipation, an integrated recognition of anarchist individualism. This individualist strand of anarchist thought, subtlety incorporated—and then advanced—in Goldman's political thinking, comprises an essential component in the anarchist critique of democracy: the opposition to majority rule.

In "The Individual, Society, and the State," Goldman declared that "more pernicious than the power of a dictator is that of a class; the most terrible—the tyranny of a majority." Goldman argued that the basis of electoral democracy—majority rule—can only restrain power, including the individual's power to act according to her needs and desires. "Real freedom, true liberty," Goldman asserted, "is positive: it is freedom to something; it is the liberty to be, to do; in short, the liberty of actual and active opportunity... [liberty that] cannot be given: it cannot be conferred by any law or government. The need of it, the longing for it, is inherent in the individual."[85] Opposed to that liberty, as Goldman stated in her essay "Majorities Versus Minorities," is "the majority, that compact, immobile, drowsy mass... [which] will always be the annihilator of individuality, of free initiative, of originality."[86]

Goldman's critique of majority rule was notably influenced by Friedrich Nietzsche,[87] but her vigilance about electoral democracy resembled that of another nineteenth-century German philosopher: Max Stirner.[88] Though first published in 1844, Stirner's writings became known to English-speaking anarchists, Goldman among them, through Benjamin Tucker's translation of *The Ego and Its Own* at the turn of the century.[89] In this book, Stirner elaborated an individualist-egoist analysis that came to articulate the anarchist aspect of individual autonomy, provoking the more communist-leaning branches of the anarchist tradition. Nevertheless, Stirner's "ontological anarchy," as political theorist Saul Newman calls it, precipitated not only the Nietzschean tradition but also post-structuralist notions of the subject as a nonessential fluid entity.[90] Stirner's critique concerned how the individual is constrained by "societies and states." Stirner targeted not only the established class but the "establishment itself, the state, not a particular state, not any such thing as the mere condition of the state at the time; it is not another state (such as a 'people's state') that men aim at, but their union, uniting, this ever-fluid uniting of everything standing."[91] His critique concerned the societal search for consensus, which Stirner read as a severe threat to individuality.

As observed by political scientist Kathy Ferguson, Goldman linked Stirner's individualism, particularly his notion of oneness, with the Nietzschean critique of morality, as outlined in *Beyond Good and Evil*.[92] Following this line of thought, Goldman attacked "the clumsy attempt of democracy to regulate the complexities of human character by means of external equality." Against these operations of democracy, Goldman drew on both Nietzsche and Stirner to suggest a vision "'beyond good and evil' [that] points to the right to oneself, to one's personality."[93]

This individualist strand of anarchist thought has clearly fostered a critique of democracy. Historian George Woodcock observed that "no conception of anarchism is further from the truth than that which regards it as an extreme form of democracy. Democracy advocates the sovereignty of the people. Anarchism advocates the sovereignty of the person."[94] One example of this critical stance came from Luigi Galleani (the Italian anarchist who advocated the targeted violence of "propaganda of the deed"). In "The End of Anarchism," Galleani followed the individualist anarchist strand of thought by declaring that "wherever possible, we must avoid, we must shun, we must reject compromise and renunciation. We must be ourselves, according to the strict character outlined by our faith and our convictions."[95] In a similar vein, Émile Armand (pseudonym of Ernest Lucien Juin) argued in his "Mini-Manual of the Anarchist Individualist" that there "is no reconciliation possible between the anarchist and any form of society built upon authority, whether it be vested in an autocrat, an aristocracy or a democracy. No common ground between the anarchist and any setting governed by the decisions of a majority or the whims of an elite."[96]

Returning again to Malatesta's critique of democracy, we find a similar drawing upon individualist approaches to majority rule. While embracing anarchist communism, yet acknowledging individual initiative, Malatesta often took a position with "the individualist anarchist of the communist school."[97] "We remain communist in our sentiment and aspiration," Malatesta wrote in his journal *Pensiero e Volantà*, "but we want to leave freedom of action to the experimentation of all ways of life that can be imagined and desired."[98] For Malatesta, the bridging of individualism and communism was guided by the notion of liberty: "the greater the possibility of communism, the greater the possibility of individualism; in other words, the greatest solidarity to enjoy the greatest liberty."[99] The aim of anarchy, Malatesta stated, "is *solidarity*, and its method is *liberty*."[100] For Malatesta, as is the case for a good part of the anarchist tradition, the means are inseparable from the ends; "one can have the most widely varying ideals when it comes to the re-making of society, but the method will always be the one that determines the goal achieved…one does not go wherever one wishes, but wherever the path one is on may lead."[101] Malatesta accordingly asserted that "whatever may be the practical results…the greatest value lies in the struggle itself."[102]

Stemming from this firm accentuation on the anarchist method, inseparable from its political goal, Malatesta attacked all forms of majority rule, understood as illegitimate coercion of individuals and minority groups. "Anarchists do not," Malatesta declared, "recognize that the majority as such, even if it were possible to establish beyond all doubt what it wanted, has the right to impose itself on the dissident minorities by the use of force."[103] It is these evaluations that led Malatesta to explore the "fundamental disagreement" between democrats and anarchists, eventually leading him to disqualify democracy altogether.[104] The anarchists, according to Errico Malatesta,

> do not wish to impose on others any hard and fast system, nor do we pretend, at least I do not, to possess the secret of a perfect social system. We wish that each social group be able, within the limits imposed by the liberty of others, to experiment on the mode of life which it believes to be the best.[105]

Here Malatesta's position resembles Bakunin's famous declaration that "I am truly free only when all human beings, men and women, are equally free. The freedom of other men, far from negating or limiting my freedom, is, on the contrary, its necessary premise and confirmation."[106] This line of thought is also notable in Kropotkin, who explicitly renounced "the idea of mutilating the individual in the name of any ideal whatsoever."[107] Accordingly, Malatesta's call for free association between individuals and groups—in place of democracy—clearly resembles his inclination to anarchist communism and the emergent strand of anarcho-syndicalism. Although Malatesta openly rejected Kropotkin's support for the entente in World War I,[108] he was nevertheless inspired by Kropotkin's communist vision on how people, after abolishing "property, government, and the state…will form themselves freely according to the necessities dictated to them by life itself."[109]

A similar link between individuality and communism was elaborated by Emma Goldman. In "Anarchism: What It Really Stands For," Goldman portrayed a "philosophy of the sovereignty of the individual." Drawing on individualist thinker Oscar Wilde, Goldman asserted that individual freedom, the cultivation of "a perfect personality…is only possible in a state of society where man is free to choose the mode of work, the conditions of work, and the freedom to work.… That being the ideal of Anarchism, its economic arrangements must consist of voluntary productive and distributive associations, gradually developing into free communism."[110] In her biography *Living My Life*, Goldman rejected the idea that social organization "means the decay of individuality." Conversely, Goldman wrote, "the true function of organization is to aid the development and growth of personality."[111] Again, we see how Goldman, like Malatesta, actively drew upon the individualist strand of anarchist thought to articulate a critique of majority rule, while simultaneously acknowledging an anarcho-communist sentiment.

Goldman accordingly opposed the urge, as she put it in one of her last writings, to "cure the evils of democracy with more democracy."[112] For Malatesta, as illustrated in our opening quote from *Neither Democrats, nor Dictators: Anarchists*, the stark denunciation of majority rule, along with representation and authority, manifests what we must recognize as an *anarchist critique* of democracy. However, anarchism also nurtures dissimilar approaches to democracy.

Anarchist Reclamation

We have seen that classical anarchism produced a profound critique of democracy. By disqualifying *authority*, the very principle of governance, the division between governors and governed becomes illegitimate. Classical anarchism further held that democracy, sealed by universal suffrage, will inevitably be managed by a small minority of elected governors through *representation*, which in turn produces unnecessary and undesirable social hierarchies. Yet even if the majority—the people—were somehow to achieve state power, classical anarchist thinkers warned that minorities, and eventually individuality itself, would be severely threatened by *majority rule*. Nevertheless, in parallel with these adamant notions of democracy's incompatibility with anarchy sprouted ideas of democracy as a trajectory, a step toward anarchy.[113] Under post-classical anarchism, these ideas have grown into what I will call an *anarchist reclamation* of democracy.

To comprehend that reclamation, we ought to consider the historiographical shift between classical and post-classical anarchism: the rise and fall of the massive anarchist movement in 1930s Spain. This historiography is indeed contentious; historian Paul Preston writes that "the Spanish Civil War is being fought all over again on paper."[114] Though not engaging with that complex set of history writing here, we shall acknowledge Preston's observation that "the Spanish Civil War was not one but many wars."[115] It is precisely in this conflictual context that the anarchist movement produced one of modern history's largest experiments with anarchy in action. Historians estimate that two-thirds of Spain's cultivated land became collectivized, some three million people were involved in autonomous rural production collectives, workers controlled a considerable number of urban factories, and anarchists ran a large proportion of the educational and welfare institutions.[116] Nonetheless, the anarchist movement eventually faced the dilemma of either joining state-oriented communist revolutionaries, which would put an end to the anarchists' autonomous collectives, or risking military defeat at the hands of General Francisco Franco.[117] The thorough attempts to build a large-scale anarchist-inspired society, while constantly defending against military invasion, were ultimately suppressed by Francoist state power. The year 1939, then, denotes the end of classical anarchism.

In the ensuing context of World War II and the unfolding bipolar geopolitics of the Cold War era, a most peculiar thing happened to democracy's genealogy in anarchist thought. While classical anarchism was concentrated on criticizing democracy, post-classical anarchism came to reclaim it.

Democracy, carried out in its pure form, was made equivalent to anarchy. The key aspiration for this radicalizing political project was, in the words of historian George Woodcock, that "orthodox democracy must give way to heretical democracy"; the dominant version of democracy thereby became distinguishable from "the notion of radical democracy."[118] The urge to reclaim "the true principles of democracy" was pointedly formulated by Herbert Read in *Poetry and Anarchism*. "If we can make politics local," Read declared, "we can make them real. For this reason the universal vote should be restricted to the local unit of government, and this local government should control all the immediate interests of the citizen."[119] As we shall see, a related proposal for "libertarian municipalism" was later elaborated by Murray Bookchin. The reading of anarchism as a struggle for "true democracy" was also noticeable in—and this is quite telling for our genealogy—Gaston Laval's influential account of the "Collectives in the Spanish Revolution," in which "democracy extended into the whole of social life."[120] Contrasted with that notion of democracy radicalized is the dominant version of democracy decorated with various pejorative adjectives. Hence, the anarchist reclamation of democracy has taken stock of democracy's participatory latency to redress, or approach, anarchy. In the following pages, we will explore anarchism's affiliation with *direct democracy* and democratic radicalization as a step *toward anarchy*.

Direct Democracy

An influential proponent of the anarchist reclamation of democracy is the linguistic scholar and anarchist theorist Noam Chomsky. Since the late 1970s, Chomsky has set out to distill meaning from the dominant form of "capitalist democracy," in which "the pump handle will generally be operated by those who control the economy."[121] This notion resonated with the anarchist tradition that, we should not forget, stems from the critical evaluation of social conflicts produced by the capitalist economy. The classical anarchists, springing from and often working in collaboration with the broader socialist movement, shared the overall notion that capitalism unequally distributes power along the lines of property ownership. "Representative democracy," declared Bakunin, "harmonizes marvelously with the capitalist economic system."[122] In this vein, Alexander Berkman specifically located democracy in a political economy that relies on capitalist ownership of the means of production. Commenting on the nascent American engagement in World War I, supposedly to "make democracy safe," Berkman declared "that a republic is not synonymous with democracy, and that America has never been a real democracy, but that it is the vilest plutocracy on the face of the globe."[123]

Departing from this classical anarchist critique of the political economy, Chomsky argued that the "state capitalist democracy has a certain tension with regard to the locus of power: in principle, the people rule, but effective power resides largely in private hands, with large-scale effects throughout the social order."[124] Echoing the political call of Mouffian radical democratic theory—though certainly not acknowledging that school—Chomsky sees potential here; corporate power could be dismantled by popular power since, as he has so pointedly put it, "democracy is a threat to any power system."[125] What is needed, therefore, is *more* democracy:

> More democracy is a value in itself. Democracy as a value doesn't have to be defended any more than freedom has to be defended. It's an essential feature of human nature that people should be free, should be able to participate, and should be un-coerced....A really meaningful democracy...would reflect my active, creative participation—not just me, but everyone, of course. That would be real democracy.[126]

Chomsky's call for "a really meaningful democracy," juxtaposed to capitalist democracy, typifies the reclamation of democracy cultivated in post-classical anarchist thought. Yet nascent versions of direct democracy had been promoted already in the era of classical anarchism. As noted by the early anarchist historian Max Nettlau, the key figure in the Spanish faction of the antiauthoritarian International, José Llunas Pujols, accentuated the necessity "to organize the administration...without any directive council or any hierarchical offices...[instead meeting] in general assembly once a week or more often...[which] prescribes a definite line of conduct for this commission or gives it an imperative mandate." Such an administrative organization, Llunas argued, "would be perfectly anarchist...[and] does not mean an abdication of that collectivity's own liberty."[127]

Nonetheless, the anarchist call for more democracy, in terms of community-based self-governance, should not be read as some anarchist capitulation to representative democracy—especially given the polarization between democracy and communism during the Cold War era. In 1945, the pioneering post-classical anarchist Paul Goodman wrote that "in small groups we must exercise direct political initiative in community problems of personal concern to ourselves (housing, community-plan, education, etc.). The constructive decisions of inmate concern to us cannot be delegated to representative government and bureaucracy."[128] Three decades later, in an essay on the possibilities of workers' councils, Maurice Joyeux similarly warned against the "centralizing temptation, either in democratic form (majority rule) or in centralist form (elite rule or vanguard party rule) will again loom as a threat. Centralization is the mechanism whereby new classes will be formed and these in turn will devise privileges that need not necessarily be economic."[129]

The reclamation of democracy, partly rooted in classical anarchism, became particularly manifest in the late twentieth century's alterglobalization movement and the succeeding Occupy movement. The alterglobalization movement seemingly answered Murray Bookchin's call from the mid-1980s to "democratize our republic and radicalize our democracy,"[130] what Amedeo Bertolo called "libertarian democracy": anarchistic face-to-face, horizontal decision-making that transcends politics of representation.[131] It was this popular wave of democratic exploration that enthused anthropologist David Graeber to announce the arrival of *The New Anarchists* in the early 2000s.[132]

In the wake of the alterglobalization movement, the anarchist version of democracy typically opposed itself to state-capitalist democracy by invoking the adjective *direct*. In the influential essay "Democracy Is Direct," Cindy Milstein illustratively argued that democracy is "completely at odds with both the state and capitalism," hence anarchists must begin "*reclaiming* the word democracy itself—not as a better version of representation but as a radical process to directly remake our world."[133]

The notion of direct democracy gained additional currency through the widespread publications of David Graeber. In *Direct Action*, Graeber argued that just as anarchists bypass the state by doing politics directly, so could democracy itself be reclaimed in the same direct manner.[134] This idea emanated from Murray Bookchin's core argument that "direct democracy is ultimately the most advanced form of direct action."[135] Bookchin formulated a critique of representative decision-making, what political theorist Uri Gordon calls an introductory "association between anarchism and democracy."[136] Bookchin advocated commune-based democracy "structured around direct, face-to-face, protoplasmic relationships, not around representative, anonymous, mechanical relationships."[137] Bookchin's *radical* notion of democracy stemmed from his reading of ancient Athens as a "working democracy in the literal sense of the term."[138] As he later came to conceptualize this approach in terms of "libertarian municipalism,"[139] further emphasis was placed on voting as a means of decision-making (which meant dissociation with the classical anarchist critique of majority rule).[140]

David Graeber, however, refrained from Bookchin's inclination to equate democracy with majority rule. In his book *The Democracy Project*, built largely on participatory observation within the North American Occupy movement,[141] Graeber explicitly juxtaposed decision-making by the vote with a consensus process.[142] Seeing that classical anarchists "tended to accept that 'democracy' meant majority voting,"[143] Graeber instead proposed an anarchist reclamation—or, more literally, a *radicalization*—of democracy in terms of consensus, "the process of collective deliberation on the principle of full and equal participation."[144] If applied with care and rigor, Graeber contended, the consensus process is unlikely to reach the point at which groups go to the vote.[145] This elucidation of consensus, though puzzlingly similar to the Habermasian vocabulary, differs overtly from the concept of deliberative (state) democracy; for Graeber, the consensus process did not only mean participation in decision-making procedures but also that "no one should be bound by a decision they detest."[146] Radicalized democracy here signifies a direct, participatory yet noncoercive political arrangement, meaning that "anarchism is not a negation of democracy [but instead]…a matter of taking those core democratic principles to their logical conclusions."[147] Noting that both democracy and anarchy have historically been used interchangeably as pejorative ascriptions, Graeber accordingly advocated their tandem reclamation.[148] Although anarchist reclamation in this vein translated into radicalization of democracy's libertarian latency, galvanized under the black flag, post-classical anarchism also developed an understanding of democracy, especially its radicalization, as a step toward anarchy.

Toward Anarchy

We have seen that anarchist reclamation of (direct) democracy was especially notable within North American factions of the late alterglobalization movement. While Occupy assemblies have indeed been recognized as a flash of anarchy in action,[149] it should be noted that parallel anarchist theorization of direct democracy has also developed aside from these phenomena. For instance, Argentinian psychoanalyst and anarchist Eduardo Colombo deliberately used the adjective "direct" to distinguish between anarchist-style democracy and the indirect, representative system associated with "capitalist-neoliberal democracy."[150] Colombo further argued that, tactically, even majority rule could, in fact, be favorable to anarchists, if the participating individuals gave their consent.[151]

At the same time, in parallel with understandings of anarchism as democracy radicalized, as opposed to the dominant form of capitalist democracy, we also encounter an anarchist approach to democracy in terms of a trajectory, a step toward anarchy. "The objective" as George Benello put it in his influential 1967 essay "We Are Caught in a Wasteland Culture," "is a society which is fully democratized."[152] Benello furthered this line of thought in the anthology *Participatory Democracy*, coedited with Dimitrios Roussopoulos. They sketched a direct and participatory democracy, modified for large-scale wage-labor societies. "Participatory democracy," they argued, "seeks to reintroduce the concept of democracy from the ground up, which means introducing democratic process into the major organizations of society, public and private."[153] This democratization is "anarchistic in its recognition that more than the democratization of the means of production and of industrial property is involved."[154] Sam Dolgoff, following that same line of thought, called for apt contextual application of anarchist principles "to stimulate forces that propel society in a libertarian direction."[155]

Here we can see the contours of democracy-as-trajectory, the notion that democracy can be a step toward anarchy. This notion has primarily been developed by Third World anarchists who have been politically active outside of the geopolitical divide of the Cold War era. For instance, Vinoba Bhave, a key ideological successor of Mohandas "Mahatma" Gandhi in post-colonial India, argued that *Sarvodaya*, the political philosophy formulated by Gandhi,[156] "does not mean good government or majority rule, it means freedom from government, it means decentralization of power.... Decisions should be taken, not by a majority, but by unanimous consent." Bhave accordingly concluded that, in the wake of the retreating British state presence, "we should not allow ourselves to be governed at all, even by a good government."[157] Another Third World anarchist thinker, surprisingly invisible in anarchist compilations,[158] is Luce Fabbri (daughter of Luigi Fabbri, Malatesta's collaborator and biographer). In Fabbri's approach to democracy, we find no contradiction between "on the one hand exposing its insufficiency, [and] on the other hand defending those spaces it keeps open."[159] Instead of opposing democracy or making it more radical, Fabbri suggested that anarchism encourages us to move beyond democracy. On the route toward anarchy, democracy becomes an important step:

> Democracy and anarchy are not mutually contradictory but the one represents an advance upon the other. In fact, there is no diametrical opposition between the rights of the majority upon which democracy is built and the free consent that is characteristic of libertarian solutions; the difference is, instead, a difference of degree.[160]

Fabbri subsequently stated that anarchists "should aim to socialize and federalize democracy and turn it into a direct, socialist democracy." Here Fabbri tuned into the idea of anarchist reclamation, emphasizing the necessity "not to defend a democratic system but rather to defend the fundamental freedoms existing within it from the assaults of totalitarian forces."[161] On a more pessimistic note, in *Two Cheers for Anarchism*, political scientist James Scott has similarly declared that we "are stuck, alas, with Leviathan, though not at all for the reasons Hobbes had supposed, and the challenge is to tame it."[162]

I would argue that this type of demarcation—today's form of democracy as unescapable yet incompatible with anarchy—is paramount to the anarchist reclamation. The anarchist writer Colin Ward put it quite clearly in his call to "build networks instead of pyramids. Anarchism does not demand the changing of the labels on the layers, it doesn't want different people on top, it wants us to clamber out from underneath. It advocates an extended network of individuals and groups, making their own decisions, controlling their own destiny."[163] In a similar vein, in his *In Defense of Anarchism*, political philosopher Robert Paul Wolff differentiated between authority and autonomy. Wolff here contended that the "defining mark of the state is authority, the right to rule. The primary obligation of man is autonomy, the refusal to be ruled."[164] Accordingly, the revolutionary content of anarchist thought, characteristically denouncing reformatory politics, fosters continuous disbelief in projects aiming to radicalize democracy.

This trajectory aspect finds clear resonance in classical anarchist thought, especially in Malatesta's notion of anarchism as a method—a process—rather than some utopian state of society. In his widely distributed pamphlet *Toward Anarchy*, written in 1899, Malatesta highlighted the fact that for anarchists what matters "is not whether we accomplish Anarchy today, tomorrow, or within ten centuries, but that we walk toward anarchy today, tomorrow, and always."[165] For Malatesta, the anarchist struggle was all about "seeking to reduce the power of the State and of privilege, and by demanding always greater freedom, greater justice."[166] Malatesta's approach, typically referred to as gradualism, ventured that "the complete triumph of anarchy will come by evolution, gradually, rather than by violent revolution."[167] This meant, for Malatesta, "that so long as government exists it should be as unoppressive as possible, the less it is a government the better."[168] At the same time, we must recall how Malatesta also formulates a most profound critique of democracy, a critique now reclaimed and debated in contemporary anarchist thought.

Reclaimed Critique

The final part of our literature review outlines how the anarchist critique of democracy has been revisited, or reclaimed, to once again target the social divide between governors and governed. However, the anarchist reclamation of democracy, the notion that "anarchism would be nothing less than the most complete realization of democracy,"[169] as Lucien van der Walt and Michael Schmidt have put it,[170] still lingers in contemporary anarchist thought. Yet voices have also been raised against democracy, revisiting the anarchist tradition in search of what we might call a *reclaimed critique of democracy*. A particularly articulate propagation of that reclaimed critique has sprung from the CrimethInc. Ex-Workers Collective think tank: "It is strange to use the word democracy for the idea that the state is inherently undesirable. The proper word for that idea is anarchism."[171] In *From Democracy to Freedom*, CrimethInc. argues that democracy in whatever form is incompatible with freedom. "Real freedom," the argument goes, "is not a question of how participatory the process of answering questions is, but of the extent to which we can frame the questions ourselves—and whether we can stop others from imposing their answers on us."[172] In formulating this argument, CrimethInc. distinguishes between government, "the exercise of authority" and the self-determination that "means disposing of one's potential on one's own terms." CrimethInc. accordingly argues that self-determination, in contrast to authority, fosters "cumulative autonomy on a mutuality reinforcing basis."[173]

CrimethInc.'s critique of democracy clearly echoes classical anarchist thought, especially the polemical writings of Errico Malatesta. As we have seen, Malatesta's argument crystalized into the notion that "the government of the people turns out to be an impossibility, [since it] can at best be only the government of the majority."[174] Similar arguments were raised in the rebellious heat of the late 1960s; in the Netherlands, for instance, the social movement known as the Provos affiliated with anarchism, a tradition that, according to the Provos, "propagates the most direct rebellion against all authority, whether it be democratic or communist."[175] Similar defiance has more recently been declared by the anarchist author Peter Gelderloos, emanating from the analysis that democracy is nothing but "a direct evolution of earlier elite institutions... creating the illusion that the subjects are in fact equal members of society."[176] Gelderloos develops this analysis in *Worshiping Power*, a study of early state formation that stems from the anarchist notion that "all forms of government, from the most dictatorial to the most democratic, are fundamentally oppressive." Gelderloos concludes that the "problem is not corruption or lack of democracy or a particular party, but the very fact that we are governed."[177] In the same vein, Uri Gordon has pronounced grave disbelief in redressing anarchism as democracy: "anarchism represents not the most radical form of democracy, but an altogether different paradigm of collective action."[178] In an essay published on CrimethInc.'s website, Gordon has argued that "anarchist invocations of democracy are a relatively new and distinctly American phenomenon." His argument is that the link between anarchism and democracy is not only ideologically incoherent but also strategically problematic since "it risks cementing the nationalist sentiments it seeks to undermine."[179] In this critical vein, the reclaimed critique of democracy has also come to include the realm of non-human life.

Democracy and Non-human Life

When the anarchist tradition is revisited in search of a critique of democracy, today's reclaimed critique also comes with additional layers. Most notably, echoing Bakunin, the reclamation of anarchist critique now encompasses the unfolding notion that democracy produces and fortifies the ruling of one class or group—or species—over another. An illustrative entry point is Mick Smith's *Against Ecological Sovereignty*, which portrays how our present political system "presumes human dominion and assumes that the natural world is already, before any decision is even made, fundamentally a human resource."[180] Smith conversely introduces anarcho-primitivism, or simply primitivism, which suggests, "in place of the political paradigm of (human) citizenship…a constitutive ecological politics of subtle involvements and relations between more-than-just-human-beings."[181] Primitivism, Smith argues, "rejects not only the commodification of nature but also the very idea of a specifically human form of labor that automatically stamps nature with a seal of proprietorship."[182] Smith's analysis acknowledges the writings of Henry David Thoreau who, in the essay "Walking," written in the late 1850s, wished "to speak a word for Nature, for absolute freedom and wildness, as contrasted with freedom and culture merely civil."[183]

Smith's analysis also draws on the anarcho-primitivism of John Zerzan, who has asserted that the state is "a hypercomplex global setup [that cannot] function a day without many levels of government."[184] Zerzan's application of this layered analysis has launched a compact critique of civilization as a whole. "Expressions of power are at the essence of civilization," Zerzan declares in *Twilight of the Machines*, only to add that civilization builds on the "core principle of patriarchal rule."[185] Green anarchism, the broader strand of contemporary anarchist thought in which anarcho-primitivism is located, unveils how the demos, even in its most radical understanding, does not encompass non-human life. Instead of embracing the logic of civilization, green anarchism evokes, as Zerzan has it, "face-to-face, non-domination of nature and each other."[186] Due to "the repression of individual liberties and the curtailment of direct action in favor of deferred decision-making rejection," green anarchists Moxie Marlinspike and Windy Hart polemically declared on primitivist Audio Anarchy Radio: "We are not echoing confused cries for more democracy, we are calling for its entire abolition."[187] Hence, the starting point for green anarchism is, as Corin Bruce bluntly puts it, "that all hierarchy should be abolished, [including] the human subordination of other species of animals."[188] Zerzan similarly declares that although "the domestication of animals and plants was once assumed as given, now its logic is brought into question."[189]

This critique of the human domestication of non-human life echoes throughout the anarchist tradition. A commonly referred to example is Élisée Reclus's pamphlet *On Vegetarianism*. Based on personal encounters with the violent exploitation of non-human animals, Reclus advocated a future "in which we no longer risk seeing butcher shops full of carcasses next to silk and jewelry stores."[190] A quite similar approach, though less frequently recounted,[191] was adopted by Louise Michel, a key organizer in the Paris Commune of 1871, later to become one of the most recognized figures within the anarchist movement.[192] In her memoirs, Michel charged the violent hierarchy between humans and animals as the ignition of her political life: "As far back as I can remember, the origin of my revolt against the powerful was my horror at the tortures inflicted on animals."[193] Michel's political struggle was located at the intersection of social inequalities, targeting the social structure in which "men are masters, and women are intermediate beings, standing between man and beast."[194] Her memoir chapter on women's rights is closely interwoven with an urge for animal rights (as branded today) and class struggle. For Michel, the principle of authority, fueling the domination of one group over another, required resistance on multiple levels. "What an uproar when men find an unruly animal in the flock. I wonder what would happen if the lamb no longer wanted to be slaughtered?"[195] Michel asked, rhetorically, in her characteristic agitation for complete defiance and the becoming of the ungovernable.

Besides Reclus and Michel, Voltairine de Cleyre seems to have shared a similar political approach. Emma Goldman reported that de Cleyre expressed "poignant agony at the sight of suffering whether of children or dumb [*sic*] animals (she was obsessed by love for the latter and would give shelter and nourishment to every stray cat and dog)."[196] These classical anarchists' theorization is now recharged in contemporary anarchism. The reclaimed critique of democracy has increasingly come to target *speciesism*: the logic through which othered species are violently exploited to produce milk and eggs, and even killed, slaughtered, their bodies transformed into food commodities for their rulers.[197]

Animal liberationist Bob Torres writes that anarchism "encourages us to see struggles as interconnected, and to act appropriately by building alliances and solidarity between them." Accordingly, Torres rejects "the consumption, enslavement, and subjugation of animals for human ends…as yet another oppressive aspect of the relations of capital and a needless form of domination."[198] Activist Brian Dominick, reflecting on his influential pamphlet *Animal Liberation and Social Revolution*, similarly conceives "both human liberation and animal freedom [as] integral aspects of anti-oppression perspective."[199] Following this line of thought, the introductory essay in *Anarchism and Animal Liberation* postulates that the anarchist tradition, "with its explicit intent of challenging and ending all forms of domination, is seen to bring something of real value, hope, and possibility."[200] Hence, the struggle against authority—the very backbone of anarchist ideas and actions—has produced a variety of implementations in situated political contexts, not least the domestication of non-human life.[201] Anarchists thereby articulate the classical critique once more, in order to evaluate ongoing searches for a more radical democracy.

Anarchy and Radical Democracy

We have seen how various strands of anarchist thought have found reason to question the *anarchist reclamation* and, in doing so, to add critique to "the radicalization of democracy."[202] The *reclaimed critique* of democracy has, in turn, nurtured subsequent discussions on the relation between democracy and anarchy. Provocative critique of radical democracy has, for instance, fueled trenchant views on the individual-community nexus.[203] In this revived debate we recognize, on the one hand, an *anarchist critique* clarifying how "anarchy describes the absence of rule, while democracy describes rule by 'the people,'"[204] and, on the other hand, an *anarchist reclamation* in which "anarchism is the most extreme, radical, form of democracy."[205] The latter argument builds not only on experiences from the Global North, such as the alter-globalization movement and its Occupy succession, but also refers to experimental democratic advances in the Global South, particularly the democratic confederalism of Kurdistan.[206] Anarchist critics of democracy dismiss such a positioning. "It is not the same thing," Uri Gordon argues, "for stateless minorities in the Global South to use the language of democracy and national liberation as it is for citizens of advanced capitalist countries in which national independence is already an accomplished fact."[207]

On a different note, contemporary anarchists have also found reason to doubt even the notion of direct and assembly-based democracy. "Sabotage every representative authority," the Invisible Committee called out in their widespread essay collection *The Coming Insurrection*; "Spread the palaver. Abolish general assemblies."[208] That sincere critique finds clear resonance in contemporary, as well as in classical, anarchist thought. "Even in most convivial communities," political philosopher Ruth Kinna points out, "individuals will organize themselves in ways that advantage some members over others. When it comes to decision-making, the more articulate, charismatic or knowledgeable are likely to dominate."[209] In this vein, CrimethInc. has construed democracy as an obstacle to free initiative, for individuals as well as for minority groups. Their analysis challenges Graeber's affirmative account of the democracy entailed in the Occupy movement; CrimethInc. has reported how the consensus process lured people into "treating it as a formal means of government—while anarchists who shared Graeber's framework found themselves outside the consensus reality of their fellow Occupiers."[210]

The contemporary anarchist critique of the direct small-scale version of democracy resembles Errico Malatesta's thinking, particularly his evaluation of the Organizational Platform of the General Union of Anarchists. The platform was initiated by several prominent anarchists, including Nestor Makhno and Peter Arshinov in 1926,[211] in the context of the emerging Bolshevik Soviet Union, where the anarchist movement in general and Makhno's militarized resistance in particular was heavily repressed.[212] Many anarchists who participated in the February Revolution in 1917 feared that the result of the Bolshevik-led October Revolution would threaten the workers' councils, the *soviets*. Gregory Maksimov, one of these critical anarchist voices, declared that the soviets "have been transformed from revolutionary organizations into organizations of stagnation, of the domination of the majority over the minority, and obstacles on the road toward the further development of progress and freedom."[213] In contrast to the Bolshevik version of democracy, Maksimov argued that "true democracy, developed to its logical extreme, can become a reality only under the conditions of a communal confederation. This democracy is Anarchy."[214]

As repression from the communist regime unfolded, Makhno and many other anarchists who took up arms against proletarian state power came to see an organizational platform as a necessity for effective resistance. Though various anarchists subscribed to this vision, many others, in particular Emma Goldman, Alexander Berkman, and, not least, Errico Malatesta, were openly critical of the platformists.[215] Malatesta elaborated his sharp critique in an open letter to Makhno: "Your organization, or your managerial organs, may be composed of anarchists but they would only become nothing other than a government."[216] In an earlier comment on the Organizational Platform, Malatesta took the opportunity to elaborate his critique of government as such:

> It is well known that anarchists do not accept majority government (democracy) any more than they accept government by the few (aristocracy, oligarchy, or dictatorship by one class or party) nor that of one individual (autocracy, monarchy, or personal dictatorship). Thousands of times anarchists have criticized so-called majority government, which anyway in practice always leads to domination by a small minority.[217]

On that same critical note, a key participant in the Makhnovist movement, Voline (Vsevolod Mikhailovich Eikhenbaum), eventually concluded that to keep a revolution alive, "it is necessary that this existence, the existing society itself, become impossible; that it be ruined from the top to bottom—its economy, its politics, its manners, customs, and prejudices."[218]

This leads us to the very *anagnorisis*, the anarchist twist, of the Impossible Argument.

The Impossible Argument

We saw in the previous chapter how the anarchist tradition has nurtured a profound critique of each and every form of governmental embodiment. Anarchism has formulated a harsh critique of authority, representation, and majority rule, but it has also construed radicalized direct democracy as synonymous with or as a step toward anarchy. In general terms, the critique of democracy typified classical anarchist thought, while the reclamation of democracy grew in the post-classical anarchism after 1939. Yet these lines of thought have coexisted historically, and they both continue into the present day. While contemporary anarchism has described anarchy in terms of radical democracy, a reclaimed critique has once again dissociated anarchy from democracy. In an attempt to recognize dialogue between them, this concluding chapter elaborates what I call the Impossible Argument.

Let us first return to our case study of how democratic conflict—the social antagonism between governors and governed—played out in Husby, the socially vigorous city district of Stockholm, and was politically condemned by the democratic state of Sweden. Here we saw that the Husby community demonstrated a dynamic and vibrant political activity; people were engaged in a variety of groups and organizations, aiming to advance local society. Using the terminology of Jacques Rancière, the radical democratic theorist who conceptualizes precisely these societal processes, *democratic life* has deeply infused the Husby community. Following the Rancièrian analysis, that democratic life subsequently produced a conflict with the *democratic state*. Over the past decades, according to interviewed Husby residents, numerous attempts have been made to influence local decision-making. The state and municipal governors, contrasted with the governed residents, have continuously ignored, disqualified, or repressed democratic life in Husby. Such a dismissive response conveys what Rancière calls "hatred of democracy"; democratic life beyond the state is seen not only as excessive but also as a direct threat to the defining contour of the democratic state: the division between governors and governed.

In the Swedish spring of 2013, that conflictual relation became markedly discernible in the streets of Husby. After the violent embodiment of the armed state—the police—was attacked, it answered with one of the most forceful police interventions in Swedish history. The people of Husby soon took to the streets to prevent further violent confrontations. When people were hurt by police batons, dog bites, and racist insults, a temporary legitimization was established: collective experiences set a local historical context for talking in defensive terms about attacking the state's armed forces. The so-called Husby riots became an intensification of an experiential historical antagonism between governors and governed. Quite tellingly, the Swedish state responded to the Husby events not by acknowledging and empowering its democratic life but by intensifying repressive measures and supplying the police with additional resources.[1] And so the conflictual antagonism between democratic life and the democratic state has continued.

Radical democratic theory as elaborated by Jacques Rancière offers an important perspective; we are given critical tools to evaluate the potential of forging democracy into a non-hierarchical project. A Rancièrian analysis of the Husby case reveals how politics beyond the state undermine the governors-governed divide, manifesting, in this exact sense, a threat to democracy. Interviewed Husby residents portrayed how they had been deprived of self-determination. One interviewee expressed this in a pointedly cynical way: "That is our beautiful democracy."[2] Such an indicative critique of democracy is indeed valuable for anyone who craves radical social change. This critique echoes throughout the anarchist tradition, eventually finding its way to the Copenhagen Summit in 2009, where our confined demonstration march sarcastically chanted: "this is what democracy looks like."

That critical take on radical democratic theory resembles, I would argue, an anarchist critique of democracy, but aside from unmasking the very boundaries of democracy, radical democratic scholars also, and this quite explicitly, defend democracy's pluralistic, direct, and participatory dimensions; the political imperative becomes a call for *more* democracy, a radicalization of what we already have. However, such a call typically translates into an inversion of the governors-governed relationship; radicalization means acknowledging the very root of democracy, namely, the people's rule (*dēmokratía*). I believe, it is precisely here that we must further our analysis: by exploring the variety of approaches to democracy offered by the sundry history of anarchist thought.

We have seen how the anarchist tradition is rather heterogeneous in its relation to democracy. Nonetheless, anarchism remains inherently skeptical of power-grabbing *within* democratic states, whatever the political intentions. This line of political thought features Rancière's theorization by exploring the very drive to escape government, to withdraw from domination—to become ungovernable.[3] In the same vein, radical democratic theorists also perceive this anarchist critique as an obstacle to political advances. Chantal Mouffe explicitly attacks what she calls "exodus theorists," polemically asking how we can pretend "that it is possible to make a revolution without taking power."[4] In place of social movement "exodus," Mouffe advocates a "profound transformation, not a desertion, of existing institutions."[5] From the Mouffian understanding of radical democracy, anarchistic politics become a most impossible argument. However, radical democratic theorization also carries alternative political imperatives. To flesh out this line of thought, this book has turned to the precise ideological tradition that advocates not left-populist urges for state power but further exploration of the *impossible*.

The notion of the "impossible" has a very special place in the anarchist tradition. Anarchism is the struggle for anarchy, a society in which domination is continuously abolished. The classical anarchist Errico Malatesta declared that "*anarchy* is a form of living together in society; a society in which people live as brothers and sisters without being able to oppress or exploit others....*Anarchism* is the method of reaching anarchy, through freedom, without government."[6] Consequently, the politics of anarchism has frequently been denounced as a naive dream, a pointless struggle for the impossible. Malatesta had already asserted in the late 1800s that "so many honest opponents believe Anarchy a thing impossible."[7] Malatesta deliberately affirmed this accusation (in line with the anarchist tradition in general) by declaring that anarchism is "always fighting to make possible what today seems impossible."[8]

This anarchist epitome is implied by the title of Peter Marshall's seminal history of anarchism *Demanding the Impossible*.[9] Yet anarchists demand nothing from those entitled to govern but, rather, from themselves. In this vein, Jacques Rancière also infers that even for anarchist predecessors in 1830s France, "the question was not to demand the impossible, but to realize it themselves."[10] Anarchism, in this respect, becomes a political struggle to challenge and extend the boundaries of political possibility.

The notion of the "impossible" also has a deeper political meaning. Anarchist struggles aim to impede and disable—to make impossible—each and every form of domination. The Impossible Argument is about making it impossible to rule. "Anarchy is our only safe polity," Paul Goodman pessimistically declared in the 1970s; "people are not to be trusted, so prevent the concentration of power."[11] More recently, the CrimethInc. Ex-Workers' Collective, endeavoring to reclaim the anarchist critique of democracy, has argued that "it is not a matter of governing in a completely participatory manner, but of making it impossible to impose any form of rule."[12] By the same token, Malatesta contended that, above all, "it must be made impossible for some to impose themselves on, and sponge off, the vast majority by material force."[13] He argued that "we want not just to improve the institutions that now exist, but to destroy them utterly, abolish all and every form of power by man over man and all parasitism, of whatever kind, on human labor."[14] To reach the political moment in which "no one may exploit anybody else's labor,"[15] and "no one could impose his wishes on others by force,"[16] Malatesta stated that anarchism seeks "to destroy every trace of privilege,"[17] but then also to "remain opposed to any embryonic government,"[18] "the re-establishment of the police and the armed forces."[19] Malatesta declared polemically: "This is our mission: demolishing, or contributing to demolish any political power whatsoever, with all the series of repressive forces that support it; preventing, or trying to prevent new governments and new repressive forces from arising."[20]

Hence, the Impossible Argument is not only about abolishing domination but also about encumbering that very tendency. This notion echoes Bakunin's call to "destroy all government and make government impossible everywhere."[21] If we are to abolish the state and the police "for good, and not see him reappear under another name and in different guise," as Malatesta pointed out, "we have to know how to live without him—that is, without violence, without oppression, without injustice, without privilege."[22] This is, I believe, a linchpin to the Impossible Argument: the construction that tandems destruction. Developing Bakunin's renowned declaration that "the desire for destruction is also a creative desire,"[23] Malatesta declared that "we must not destroy anything that satisfies human need however badly—until we have something better to put in its place."[24] If not, Malatesta warned, "we shall leave such matters to the 'leaders' and we shall have a new government."[25]

This tandem characteristic of anarchist resistance—the entanglement of destruction and construction—echoes throughout the anarchist tradition. Kropotkin, for one, emphasized that "it is not enough to destroy. We must also know how to build."[26] Inspired by Kropotkin's writings, the pamphlet *Declaration of the Korean Revolution*, authored by Shin Chaeho in 1923,[27] similarly declared that "we destroy in order not just to destroy but to construct. If we do not know how to construct, that means we do not know how to destroy... destruction and construction are inseparable, not two but one."[28] The urge to destroy, to "smash all forms of domination," as anarcha-feminist Carol Ehrlich put it in the late 1970s, "is not just a slogan, it is the hardest task of all. It means that we have to see through the spectacle, destroy the stage sets, know that there are other ways of doing things."[29] This very notion, today most commonly recognized in terms of prefigurative politics,[30] was particularly crystallized by Gustav Landauer: "The state is a social relationship; a certain way of people relating to one another. It can be destroyed by creating new social relationships; i.e., by people relating to one another differently."[31] Landauer thereby construed state and capital as sets of relations;[32] meaning that destruction becomes inseparable from the process of creation.

This constructive notion has been particularly elaborated by spiritual and religious branches of the anarchist tradition.[33] It became a key notion of the anarcho-pacifism recognizable in Bart de Ligt's famous aphorism from the mid-1930s: "the greater the violence, the weaker the revolution."[34] This vein of radical pacifism was particularly elaborated through the politico-theological thinking of the Russian writer Lev Tolstoy.[35] Following the anarchist assumption that "there could not be worse violence than that of Authority,"[36] Tolstoy craved complete government abolition, calling for "neither congresses nor conferences, nor treaties, nor courts of arbitration, but the destruction of those instruments of violence which are called Governments, and from which humanity's greatest evils flow."[37] Hence the guiding idea for Tolstoyan anarcho-pacifism was that government must be resisted "not in setting up fresh violence, but in abolishing whatever renders governmental violence possible."[38]

The Impossible Argument, then, calls for permanent abolishment of all forms of government—which invokes a continuous impeding of authority growing anew. While this stance allows for a critique of democracy, such a critique is rather impossible to articulate within a democratic discourse. As I have tried to show in this book, anarchism has dealt with this particular dilemma for quite some time.

On the one hand, the call for political self-determination and direct action puts anarchism in resonance with the participatory dimension of democracy. An anarchist reclamation of democracy carries the valuable benefit of escaping pejorative accusations of being too eccentric or unreasonable. By recontextualizing anarchism as *radical* democracy, it becomes possible to formulate a powerful critique of today's state-capitalist democracy. Furthermore, the radical democratic notion of allowing dissensus, in contrast to Habermas's deliberative democratic model aimed at consensus-seeking, is indeed reflected in anarchist thought. Geographer Simon Springer argues that "an anarchic model of radical democracy, where agonism replaces antagonism, is precisely the realization of non-violent politics."[39] CrimethInc. has, in this vein, suggested that councils and assemblies could function not as miniature government bodies but as "spaces of encounter," dynamic fora that allow "for differences to arise, conflicts to play out, and transformations to occur as different social constellations converge and diverge."[40] Hence, by recognizing the pluralist and participatory dimensions of democracy, understood in spatial rather than political terms, anarchism aligns with open-ended explorations into a more radical democracy.

On the other hand, anarchist thought has also acknowledged accusations of being anti-democratic. Classical anarchism opposed democracy for its reliance on *authority*, a principle of domination establishing an undesirable and unnecessary social hierarchy—a division between governors and governed. Contemporary anarchist thought has also warned that whenever democracy extends the defining boundaries of the demos, other individuals, groups, or species will inevitably be excluded. The critique of *representative* democracy has a long tradition in feminist-leaning anarchism and the critique of *majority rule* in egoist anarchism. The anarchist critique of democracy finds resonance with Rancière's notion of endemic conflict between democratic life and the democratic state. Then again, for Rancière, democracy also means political inversion; it asserts "the power of the people, which is not the power of the population or of the majority, but the power of anyone at all."[41] Though subversive and threatening to those in power, this people's rule does not challenge the deeper political setting. Conversely, Miguel Abensour's radical democratic theorization armors an "insurgent democracy" with "the possibility of annihilating the division between governors and governed, or of reducing it to almost nothing."[42] In Husby, where residents were excluded from democratic decision-making procedures, the immediate political response would, by this token, be to extend the demos by also including those located at the margins of society. Radicalizing democracy could here translate into locally rooted political influence. An anarchist critique of democracy, however, goes deeper: it attacks the motor of democratic conflict, the antagonism between government and those it tries to govern; it demands nothing less than making governmental rule impossible.

The Impossible Argument instigates destruction of institutions and practices to make ruling possible, while at the same time fostering construction of alternative sets of social relations that impede authority from growing anew. It disqualifies the very political prerequisites of democracy, the struggle over which group will rule over the other. I believe this line of thought may guide us further—past democracy and toward anarchy. Anarchism cultivates a vigorous demand for what is now impossible: a free world of many worlds, so far from yet so very near to the world as we know it today. To make impossible any embodiment of domination, anarchy must be practiced in the here and now. Surely, such an endeavor to organize society beyond the state will, as sorely experienced in Husby, become a threat to those who attempt to govern others. In this respect, we have much more to learn from popular struggles through which people become and remain ungovernable.

Notes

The Search for Radical Democracy

1   Joseph Schumpeter, *Capitalism, Socialism and Democracy* (New York: Routledge, 2005 [1943]), 269–73.
2   Boaventura De Sousa Santos and Leonardo Avritzer, "Introduction: Opening up the Canon of Democracy," in *Democratizing Democracy: Beyond the Liberal Democratic Canon*, ed. Boaventura de Sousa Santos (London: Verso, 2005), xxxiv–li; Graham Smith, *Democratic Innovations: Designing Institutions for Citizen Participation* (Cambridge: Cambridge University Press, 2009).
3   Robert Dahl, *On Democracy* (New Haven: Yale University Press, 1998), 10.
4   See Robert Putnam, Robert Leonardi, and Raffaella Nanetti, *Making Democracy Work: Civic Traditions in Modern Italy* (Princeton: Princeton University Press, 1993), 182.
5   David Trend, "Democracy's Crisis of Meaning," in *Radical Democracy: Identity, Citizenship and the State*, ed. David Trend (London: Routledge, 1995).
6   Lars Tønder and Lasse Thomassen, "Introduction: Rethinking Radical Democracy between Abundance and Lack," ed. Lars Tønder and Lasse Thomassen (Manchester: Manchester University Press, 2005), 3–5; also see David Trend, "Introduction," in ibid., 2–3.
7   Chantal Mouffe, "Preface: Democratic Politics Today," in *Dimensions of Radical Democracy: Pluralism, Citizenship, Community*, ed. Chantal Mouffe (London: Verso, 1992), 1.
8   See Seyla Benhabib, "Introduction: The Democratic Moment and the Problem of Difference," in *Democracy and Difference: Contesting the Boundaries of the Political*, ed. Seyla Benhabib (Princeton: Princeton University Press, 1996), 6–8; Aletta Norval, "Radical Democracy," in *Encyclopedia of Democratic Thought*, ed. Paul Barry Clarke and Joe Foweraker (New York: Routledge, 2001), 587–90.
9   Ernesto Laclau and Chantal Mouffe, *Hegemony and Socialist Strategy: Towards a Radical Democratic Politics* (London: Verso, 2001 [1985]), xvii–xviii, 159–71.
10   Adrian Little and Moya Lloyd, "Introduction," in *The Politics of Radical Democracy*, ed. Adrian Little and Moya Lloyd (Edinburgh: Edinburgh University Press, 2009), 1–7.
11   See, for instance, Tønder and Thomassen, "Introduction: Rethinking Radical Democracy Between Abundance and Lack," 3–5.

12   Douglas Lummis, *Radical Democracy* (Ithaca: Cornell University Press, 1996), 27.
13   Ernesto Laclau, *On Populist Reason* (London: Verso, 2005), 249.
14   Mouffe, "Preface: Democratic Politics Today," 11.
15   See discussion in Anna Marie Smith, *Laclau and Mouffe: The Radical Democratic Imaginary* (London: Routledge, 1998), 30–35.
16   Chantal Mouffe, *Agonistics: Thinking of the World Politically* (London: Verso, 2013), 66–71.
17   Ibid., 76–77.
18   Ibid., 126.
19   Marianne Maeckelbergh, *The Will of the Many: How the Alterglobalisation Movement Is Changing the Face of Democracy* (London: Pluto Press, 2009), 29–40, 140.
20   David Graeber, "The New Anarchists," *New Left Review* 13, no. 13 (January 2002): 70.
21   Barbara Epstein, "Radical Democracy and Cultural Politics: What About Class? What About Political Power?" in Trend, *Radical Democracy*, 136.
22   See, for instance, Moya Lloyd, "Performing Radical Democracy," in Little and Moya, *The Politics of Radical Democracy*, 48–50; Birgit Schippers, "Judith Butler, Radical Democracy and Micro-politics," in ibid., 75–77.
23   Mouffe, *Agonistics: Thinking of the World Politically* (London: Verso, 2013), 91–94, 119–23.
24   Ernesto Laclau, "The Future of Radical Democracy," in Tønder and Thomassen, *Radical Democracy*, 261.
25   Simon Critchley, "True Democracy: Marx, Political Subjectivity and Anarchic Meta-Politics," ibid., 229.
26   Ibid., 232.
27   Miguel Abensour, *Democracy against the State: Marx and the Machiavellian Moment* (Cambridge: Polity, 2011 [1997]), xxiii, 97.
28   Jacques Rancière, *Hatred of Democracy* (London: Verso, 2006), 49.
29   Ibid., 29.
30   Ibid., 94.
31   Abensour, *Democracy against the State*, xl, 100.

Anti-Police Riots in Sweden

1   For empirical details, see my chapter contribution in the research anthology presenting our results; Markus Lundström, "Det demokratiska hotet," in *Bortom kravallerna: Konflikt, tillhörighet och representation i Husby*, ed. Paulina de los Reyes and Magnus Hörnqvist (Stockholm: Stockholmia, 2016).
2   See Kristina Boréus, "Husbyhändelserna i nyheter och politisk debatt," ibid.
3   Our approach was deeply inspired by the rigorous, though far more resourceful, British research project *Reading the Riots*; see Paul Lewis, Tim Newburn, Matthew Taylor, Catriona McGillivray, Aster Greenhill, Harold Frayman, and Rob N. Proctor, *Reading the Riots: Investigating England's Summer of Disorder* (London: Guardian/LSE, 2011), accessed August 15, 2022, http://eprints.lse.ac.uk/id/eprint/46297. For an in-depth discussion of our critical research methodology, see Paulina de Los Reyes and Markus Lundström, "Researching Otherwise? Autoethnographic Notes on the 2013 Stockholm Riots," *Critical*

Sociology 47, nos. 7–8 (November 2021), accessed August 15, 2022, https://doi.org/10.1177/0896920520978482.

4   However, the police eventually represented the largest source in media reports, despite the dense journalist presence in Husby; see Kristina Boréus, "Husbyhändelserna i nyheter och politisk debatt," in De los Reyes and Hörnqvist, *Bortom kravallerna*, 74–75.

5   "The Järva Vision" (2016), accessed September 26, 2016, unavailable August 11, 2022, http://bygg.stockholm.se/Alla-projekt/Jarvalyftet/In-English.

6   Interview no. 2, June 26, 2013, in Husby.

7   *Husby kräver respect* (Husby Demands Respect) (press release), January 2012.

8   Paulina de Los Reyes, "Husby, våldet och talandets villkor," in De los Reyes and Hörnqvist, *Bortom kravallerna*.

9   Cited in ibid., 168.

10   See Boréus, "Husbyhändelserna i nyheter och politisk debatt," in ibid.

11   Ove Sernhede, Catharina Thörn, and Håkan Thörn, "The Stockholm Uprising in Context: Urban Social Movements in the Rise and Demise of the Swedish Welfare-State City," in *Urban Uprisings: Challenging Neoliberal Urbanism in Europe*, ed. Margit Mayer, Catharina Thörn, and Håkan Thörn (London: Palgrave Macmillan, 2016), 64–66, 150; Carl-Ulrik Schierup, Aleksandra Ålund, and Lisa Kings, "Reading the Stockholm Riots: A Moment for Social Justice?" *Race & Class* 55, no. 3 (January 2014): 1.

12   De Los Reyes, "Husby, våldet och talandets villkor," in De los Reyes and Hörnqvist *Bortom kravallerna*.

13   Interview no. 18, June 24, 2013, in Husby.

14   Interview no. 11, June 20, 2013, in Husby.

15   Magnus Hörnqvist, "Riots in the Welfare State: The Contours of a Modern-Day Moral Economy," *European Journal of Criminology* 13, no. 5 (September 2016).

16   Joshua Clover, *Riot. Strike. Riot: The New Era of Uprisings* (London: Verso, 2016), 47, 150–52.

17   Sernhede, Thörn, and Thörn, "The Stockholm Uprising in Context, 163.

18   Interview no. 29, August 7, 2013, in Husby.

19   Kristina Boréus and Janne Flyghed, "Poliskultur på kollisionskurs," in De los Reyes and Hörnqvist, *Bortom kravallerna*.

20   Interview no. 7, June 20, 2013, in Husby.

21   Interview no. 3, June 12, 2013, in Husby.

22   Alejandro Gonzalez, "Husby, mostånd och gemenskap," in De los Reyes and Hörnqvist, *Bortom kravallerna*.

23   Interview no. 1, June 20, 2013, in Husby.

24   Interview no. 13, July 1, 2013, in Kista.

25   Interview no. 1.

26   Interview no. 11.

27   Gonzalez, "Husby, mostånd och gemenskap," in in De los Reyes and Hörnqvist, *Bortom kravallerna*.

28   Cited in Boréus, "Husbyhändelserna i nyheter och politisk debatt," in ibid., 90.

29   On May 21, after two intense nights of violent confrontations in Husby, Prime Minister Fredrik Reinfeldt officially declared his antipathy for "groups of young men who believe they can and should change society with violent means."

The police, less subtle still, stated that "stone-throwers pose a severe threat to democracy. We are here to stay!"; see Lundström, "Det demokratiska hotet," in ibid. 27.

30   Paulina De Los Reyes and Magnus Hörnqvist, "Introduktion. Konflikt, tillhörighet och representation," in ibid.
31   Marcus Lauri, "Vad är problemet med Husby?" in ibid.
32   Jacques Rancière, *Hatred of Democracy* (London: Verso, 2006), 29.
33   Interview no. 26, August 7, 2013, in Husby.
34   Interview no. 6, June 26, 2013, in Husby.

Anarchism and Democracy

1   Pierre-Joseph Proudhon, *General Idea of the Revolution in the Nineteenth Century* (New York: Haskell House Publishers, 1969 [1851]), 294.
2   Kanno Sugako, "Kanno Sugako" (1911), in *Reflections on the Way to the Gallows: Rebel Women in Prewar Japan*, ed. Mikiso Hane (Berkeley: University of California Press, 1988), 67–68.
3   Montseny, 1931; cited in Juan Gómez Casas, *Anarchist Organisation: The History of the F.A.I.* (Montréal: Black Rose Books, 1986), 157.
4   Charlotte Wilson, "Anarchism" (1886), in *Quiet Rumours: An Anarcha-Feminist Reader*, 3rd ed., ed. Dark Star Collective (Oakland: AK Press, 2012), 90.
5   Voltairine De Cleyre, "The Making of an Anarchist" (1903), in *The Voltairine de Cleyre Reader*, ed. A. J. Brigati (Oakland: AK Press, 2004), 106.
6   Emma Goldman, "Some More Observations (Free Society, April 29, 1900)," in *Emma Goldman: A Documentary History of the American Years, Volume 1: Made for America, 1890–1901*, ed. Candace Falk (Berkeley: University of California Press, 2003), 402.
7   Goldman, "The Law's Limit (New York World, October 17, 1893)," in ibid., 182.
8   Paul Avrich and Karen Avrich, *Sasha and Emma: The Anarchist Odyssey of Alexander Berkman and Emma Goldman* (Cambridge: Harvard University Press, 2012), 156–62; Candace Falk, "Forging Her Place: An Introduction," in *Emma Goldman: A Documentary History of the American Years, Volume 1*, 73–81.
9   As observed by Kathy Ferguson, the label launched by President J. Edgar Hoover, in fact, displayed Goldman, along with Alexander Berkman, as "two of the most dangerous anarchists in America." Ferguson argues that the shift from "anarchist" to "woman" in the public image of dangerous individuals served not only to downplay Goldman's political affiliation but also to dislocate the severe violence against laborers in the US; Kathy Ferguson, *Emma Goldman: Political Thinking in the Streets* (Lanham: Rowman & Littlefield, 2011), 21–29, 44–57.
10   Candace Falk, "Forging Her Place: An Introduction," in *Emma Goldman: A Documentary History of the American Years. Volume 1*, 6-7; also see Sharon Presley and Crispin Sartwell, *Exquisite Rebel: The Essays of Voltairine de Cleyre—Anarchist, Feminist, Genius* (New York: State University of New York Press, 2005), 47; Vivian Gornick, *Emma Goldman: Revolution as a Way of Life* (New Haven: Yale University Press, 2011), 14–17.
11   See Paul Avrich, *The Haymarket Tragedy* (Princeton: Princeton University Press, 1984), 181–215.
12   Ferguson, *Emma Goldman*, 133–38.

13   Maia Ramnath, *Decolonizing Anarchism: An Antiauthoritarian History of India's Liberation Struggle* (Oakland: AK Press, 2011), 6.

14   See Mike Finn, *Debating Anarchism: A History of Action, Ideas and Movements* (London: Bloomsbury, 2021); Carissa Honeywell, *Anarchism* (Cambridge: Polity, 2021).

15   Benedict Anderson, *Under Three Flags: Anarchism and the Anti-Colonial Imagination* (London: Verso, 2005), 2.

16   Ferguson, *Emma Goldman*, 229–37.

17   Paul Eltzbacher, *Anarchism: Seven Exponents of the Anarchist Philosophy* (London: Freedom Press, 1960 [1911]); Max Nettlau, *A Short History of Anarchism* (London: Freedom Press, 2000 [1932]); George Woodcock, *Anarchism: A History of Libertarian Ideas and Movements* (Cleveland: World Publishing Company, 1962); Peter Marshall, *Demanding the Impossible: A History of Anarchism* (London: Harper Perennial, 2008 [1992]); Ruth Kinna, *The Government of No One: The Theory and Practice of Anarchism* (London: Pelican, 2019).

18   See, for instance, Jesse Cohn, *Underground Passages: Anarchist Resistance Culture, 1848–2011* (Oakland: AK Press, 2015); Iwona Janicka, *Theorizing Contemporary Anarchism: Solidarity, Mimesis and Radical Social Change* (London: Bloomsbury, 2017).

19   Markus Lundström, "'The Ballot Humbug': Anarchist Women and Women's Suffrage," *Moving the Social: Journal of Social History and the History of Social Movements* 66 (2022).

20   See, for instance, Penny Weiss and Loretta Kensinger, *Feminist Interpretations of Emma Goldman* (Pennsylvania: Penn State Press, 2007). The content of Goldman's contribution is, however, still debated. Some of Goldman's readers would agree with Vivian Gornick (*Emma Goldman*, 140) that "Emma Goldman was not a thinker; she was an incarnation. It was not her gift for theory or even strategy made her memorable; it was the extraordinary force of life in her that burned, without rest or respite, on behalf of human integrity." Other readers, myself included, stress Goldman's innovative ability to synthesize different strands of anarchist—and extra-anarchist—thought into her own political thinking, which Kathy Ferguson (*Emma Goldman*, 5–6) conceptualizes as "a *located* register: it is situated, event-based and concrete." In addition to Ferguson's observation that Goldman breached the theory-practice dualism, I would argue that her open acknowledgment of individualist thought fueled the anarchist critique, not only of the state communism to come but of the democratic state itself.

21   Ferguson, *Emma Goldman*, 268.

22   For an intriguing critical discussion on this theme, see Ruth Kinna and Süreyyya Evren, *Blasting the Canon* (New York: Punctum Books, 2013), especially Michelle Campbell, ibid., 75–77, which argues for canonizing Voltairine de Cleyre for her pioneering urge for "anarchism without adjectives."

23   For further reading, see the scientific journal *Anarchist Studies* or the introductory overview of this scholarly field in Randall Amster, Abraham DeLeon, Luis Fernandez, Anthony J. Nocella, and Deric Shannon, *Contemporary Anarchist Studies: An Introductory Anthology of Anarchy in the Academy* (London: Routledge, 2009).

24 Vernon Richards, "Notes for a Biography," in *Errico Malatesta: His Life and Ideas*, ed. Vernon Richards (London: Freedom Press, 1965), 237–40; Marshall, *Demanding the Impossible*, 346–50.

25 Historian Robert Graham makes a similar observation, though also including Herbert Read therein; Robert Graham, "Preface," in *Anarchism: A Documentary History of Libertarian Ideas, Vol. 1, From Anarchy to Anarchism (300CE to 1939)*, ed. Robert Graham (Montréal: Black Rose Books, 2005), xiii.

26 Errico Malatesta, "From a Matter of Tactics to a Matter of Principle" (1897), in *The Method of Freedom: An Errico Malatesta Reader*, ed. Davide Turcato (Oakland: AK Press, 2014), 216.

27 Errico Malatesta, "Neither Democrats, nor Dictators: Anarchists" (1926), in *The Anarchist Revolution: Polemical Articles 1924–1931*, ed. Vernon Richards (London: Freedom Press, 1995), 76.

28 Malatesta defined *gendarme* as "any armed force, any material force in the service of a man or of a class, to oblige others to do what they would otherwise not do voluntarily"; see Errico Malatesta, "Article Excerpt From *Umanità Nova*, July 25, 1920," in *Errico Malatesta: His Life and Ideas*, ed. Vernon Richards (London: Freedom Press, 1965), 26.

29 Malatesta, "Neither Democrats, nor Dictators," 74.

30 Malatesta, "Anarchy" (1891), in Turcato, *The Method of Freedom*, 113.

31 Élisée Reclus, "The Modern State" (1905), in *Anarchy, Geography, Modernity: Selected Writings of Elisée Reclus*, ed. John Clark and Camille Martin (Oakland: PM Press, 2013), 189.

32 Proudhon, *General Idea of the Revolution in the Nineteenth Century*, 294.

33 Pierre-Joseph Proudhon, *What Is Property? An Inquiry into the Principle of Right and of Government* (New York: Dover Publications, 1970 [1840]), 271–72.

34 Ibid., 277. Proudhon's understanding of anarchism in the sense of order, (in) famously portrayed as a circled A, was very much indebted to the pre-Marxian socialism of Charles Fourier and Henri de Saint-Simon; see George Woodcock, *Pierre-Joseph Proudhon: A Biography* (Montréal: Black Rose Books, 1987 [1956]), 40–41.

35 Mikhail Bakunin, "Federalism, Socialism, Anti-Theologism" (1867), in *Bakunin on Anarchy: Selected Works by the Activist-Founder of World Anarchism*, ed. Sam Dolgoff (London: Routledge, 2013), 133.

36 Mikhail Bakunin, "The Illusion of Universal Suffrage" (1870), in *Democracy: A Reader*, ed. Ricardo Blaug and John Schwarzmantel (New York: Columbia University Press, 2016), 167–69.

37 Errico Malatesta, "Article Excerpt From *Pensiero e Volantà*, July 1, 1926," in *Errico Malatesta: His Life and Ideas*, ed. Richards (London: Freedom Press, 1965), 209.

38 Malatesta, "An Anarchist Programme," in Turcato, *The Method of Freedom*, 289.

39 Charlotte Wilson, "The Principles and Aims of Anarchists" (1886), in *Quiet Rumours: An Anarcha-Feminist Reader*, 3rd ed., ed. Dark Star Collective (Oakland: AK Press, 2012), 91.

40 Wilson, "Social Democracy and Anarchism," in ibid., 84.

41 Mikhail Bakunin, "What Is the State"(1869), in Graham, *Anarchism: A Documentary History of Libertarian Ideas, Vol. 1*, 86–87.

42 Mikhail Bakunin, "Statism and Anarchy" (1873), in *Bakunin on Anarchy: Selected Works by the Activist-Founder of World Anarchism*, ed. Sam Dolgoff (London: Routledge, 2013), 328, 338.

43 Reclus, "Anarchy" (1894), in Clark and Martin, *Anarchy, Geography, Modernity*, 121.

44 Proudhon, *What Is Property?* 33.

45 Proudhon, *General Idea of the Revolution in the Nineteenth Century*, 126.

46 Luigi Fabbri, "Fascism: The Preventive Counter-Revolution" (1921), in Graham, *Anarchism: A Documentary History of Libertarian Ideas, Vol. 1*, 414.

47 A few additional people from the international anarchist movement partook in this alliance, among them Giuseppe Fanelli and Alberto Tucci; see Josep Termes, *Anarquismo y sindicalismo en España: La Primera Internacional (1864–1881)* (Barcelona: Crítica, 2000 [1977]), 14; Max Nettlau, *A Short History of Anarchism* (London: Freedom Press, 2000 [1932]), 115–16.

48 Bakunin, "Revolutionary Catechism" (1866), in Dolgoff, *Bakunin on Anarchy*, 96.

49 As does Robert Cutler in his introduction to Bakunin's thought; Robert Cutler, "Introduction," in Mikhail Bakunin, *From Out of the Dustbin: Bakunin's Basic Writings 1869–1871*, ed. Robert Cutler (Ann Arbor: Ardis, 1985), 27–28.

50 Robert Graham, "Democracy and Anarchy," March 6, 2017, Robert Graham's Anarchism Weblog, accessed August 12, 2022, https://robertgraham.wordpress.com/2017/06/03/robert-graham-anarchy-and-democracy.

51 Mikhail Bakunin, "Letter to the Internationalists of the Romagna" (1872), in "Colin Ward: The Anarchist Contribution," in *Participatory Democracy: Prospects for Democratizing Democracy*, ed. Dimitrios Roussopoulos and George Benello (Montréal: Black Rose Books, 2005), 247–48.

52 Bakunin, "The Program of the Alliance" (1871), in Dolgoff, *Bakunin on Anarchy*, 257. It should be noted that radical democratic theorist Miguel Abensour clearly subscribes to the Bakunist logic by arguing that "democracy can only exist inasmuch as it rises *against* the state"; yet Abensour extracts that political line of thought from Bakunin's key adversary: Karl Marx; Miguel Abensour, *Democracy against the State: Marx and the Machiavellian Moment* (Cambridge: Polity, 2011 [1997]), xxxii–xxxiii.

53 Proudhon, *General Idea of the Revolution in the Nineteenth Century*, 128.

54 Ibid., 135.

55 For an informative in-depth analysis of the intertwined biography of these prominent anarchist figures, see Avrich and Avrich, *Sasha and Emma*.

56 Alexander Berkman, "Apropos," *Mother Earth Bulletin*, no. 1 (October 1917).

57 Bakunin, "God and the State" (1871), in Dolgoff, *Bakunin on Anarchy*, 231.

58 Nettlau, *A Short History of Anarchism*, 18–21.

59 Marshall, *Demanding the Impossible*, 191.

60 Woodcock, *Anarchism*, 60.

61 William Godwin, "Enquiry Concerning Political Justice and Its Influence on Morals and Happiness" (1793), in *Romantic Rationalist: A William Godwin Reader*, ed. Peter Marshall (Oakland: PM Press, 2017), 68, 70.

62 George Woodcock, "Democracy, Heretical and Radical" (1970), in Roussopoulos and Benello, *Participatory Democracy*, 19–20.

63   Wilson, "Social Democracy and Anarchism," in Dark Star Collective, *Quiet Rumours*, 83–84.

64   Bakunin, "Statism and Anarchy," 330–31.

65   Bakunin, "On Representative Government and Universal Suffrage" (1870), in Dolgoff, *Bakunin on Anarchy*, 220–21.

66   Malatesta, "The Socialists and the Elections: A Letter from E. Malatesta" (1897), in Turcato, *The Method of Freedom*, 210.

67   Pyotr Kropotkin, *Modern Science and Anarchism* (London: Freedom Press, 1912), 68.

68   James Guillaume, "Michael Bakunin: A Biographical Sketch" (1907), in Dolgoff, *Bakunin on Anarchy*, 50–51.

69   Carlo Cafiero, "Anarchy and Communism" (1880), in *No Gods No Masters: An Anthology of Anarchism*, ed. Daniel Guérin (Oakland: AK Press, 2005), 294.

70   Lucy Parsons, "The Ballot Humbug: A Delusion and a Snare; a Mere Veil Behind which Politics Is Played" (1905), in *Lucy Parsons: Freedom, Equality & Solidarity: Writings & Speeches, 1878–1937*, ed. Roxanne Dunbar-Ortiz (Chicago: Charles H. Kerr, 2004), 95.

71   He Zhen, "Problems of Women's Liberation" (1907), in Graham, *Anarchism: A Documentary History of Libertarian Ideas. Vol. 1*, 340–41.

72   Peter Zarrow, *Anarchism and Chinese Political Culture* (New York: Columbia University Press, 1990), 49–55, 130; Peter Zarrow, "He Zhen and Anarcho-Feminism in China," *Journal of Asian Studies* 47, no. 4 (November 1988): 808–11.

73   Malatesta, "Democracy and Anarchy" (1924), in Richards, *The Anarchist Revolution*, 78.

74   Lundström, "The Ballot Humbug."

75   Emma Goldman, "Letter to Stella Ballantine" (1919), in *Emma Goldman: Political Thinking in the Streets*, ed. Kathy Ferguson (Lanham: Rowman & Littlefield, 2011), 257.

76   Gornick, *Emma Goldman*, 75.

77   Voltairine De Cleyre, "The Political Equality of Woman" (1894), in *Exquisite Rebel: The Essays of Voltairine De Cleyre: Feminist, Anarchist, Genius*, ed. Sharon Presley and Crispin Sartwell (New York: State University of New York Press, 2005), 241–43.

78   See Andrea Pakieser, *I Belong Only to Myself: The Life and Writings of Leda Rafanelli* (Oakland: AK Press, 2014).

79   See Martha Ackelsberg, *Free Women of Spain: Anarchism and the Struggle for the Emancipation of Women* (Oakland: AK Press, 2005 [1991]), 115–20, 226–27.

80   Federica Montseny (1924), cited in Shirley Fredricks, "Feminism: The Essential Ingredient in Federica Montseny's Anarchist Theory," in *European Women on the Left: Socialism, Feminism, and the Problems Faced by Political Women, 1880 to the Present*, ed. Jane Slaughter and Robert Kern (Westport: Greenwood Press, 1981), 133.

81   Emma Goldman, "Woman Suffrage" (1911), in *Red Emma Speaks*, ed. Alix Kates Schulman (Amherst: Humanity Books, 1998), 190, 92.

82   Ibid., 192–93, 202.

83   Cited in Fredricks, "Feminism: The Essential Ingredient in Federica Montseny's Anarchist Theory," in Slaughter and Kern, *European Women on the Left*, 130.

84   Parsons, "The Ballot Humbug," 96–97.

85   Goldman, "The Individual, Society and the State" (1940), in Schulman, *Red Emma Speaks*, 121.

86   Goldman, "Minorities Versus Majorities" (1911), in Schulman, *Red Emma Speaks*, 83, 85.

87   See, for instance, Emma Goldman, *Living My Life: Two Volumes in One* (New York: Cosimo, 2011 [1931]), 191–93.

88   Falk, "Forging Her Place: An Introduction," in Falk, *Emma Goldman*, 10–11; Kathy Ferguson, "Why Anarchists Need Stirner," in *Max Stirner*, ed. Saul Newman (Basingstoke: Palgrave Macmillan, 2011), 172–73.

89   See David Leopold, "A Solitary Life," in Newman, *Max Stirner*, 36.

90   Saul Newman, "Introduction: Re-encountering Stirner's Ghosts," in ibid., 1–10; Saul Newman, *Postanarchism* (Cambridge: Polity Press, 2016).

91   Max Stirner, *The Ego and Its Own* (Cambridge: Cambridge University Press, 1995 [1870]), 198–99.

92   Ferguson, *Emma Goldman*, 161–62.

93   Goldman, "Jealousy: Causes and a Possible Cure" (1915), in Schulman, *Red Emma Speaks*, 215.

94   Woodcock, *Anarchism*, 33.

95   Luigi Galleani, "The End of Anarchism" (1907) in Graham, *Anarchism: A Documentary History of Libertarian Ideas, Vol. 1*, 122.

96   Émile Armand, "Mini-Manual of the Anarchist Individualist" (1911), in Graham, *Anarchism: A Documentary History of Libertarian Ideas, Vol. 1*, 146.

97   Errico Malatesta, "Individualism in Anarchism" (1897), in *The Complete Works of Malatesta, Vol. 3, A Long and Patient Work: The Anarchist Socialism of L'Agitazione, 1897–1898*, ed. Davide Turcato (Oakland: AK Press, 2016), 80.

98   Malatesta, "Individualism and Anarchism" (1924), in Turcato, *The Method of Freedom*, 461.

99   Malatesta, "Communism and Individualism (Comment on an Article by Max Nettlau)" (1926), in Richards, *The Anarchist Revolution*, 16.

100   Malatesta, "Anarchy" (1891), in Turcato, *The Method of Freedom*, 143.

101   Malatesta, "Our Plans: Union between Communists and Collectivists" (1899), in ibid., 99.

102   Malatesta, "An Anarchist Programme" (1899), in ibid., 287.

103   Malatesta, "Article Excerpt from *Umanità Nova*, October 6, 1921," in *Errico Malatesta*, 73.

104   Malatesta, "Collectivism, Communism, Socialist Democracy and Anarchism," in *The Complete Works of Malatesta, Vol. 3*, 237. It should be noted that Malatesta followed a most common understanding of democracy: "government of the people ruling through their freely elected representatives"; Malatesta, "Republic and Revolution" (1924), in Richards, *The Anarchist Revolution*, 37.

105   Errico Malatesta, "Violence as a Social Factor" (1895), in Graham, *Anarchism: A Documentary History of Libertarian Ideas. Vol. 1*, 163.

106   Bakunin, "God and the State" (1871), in Dolgoff, *Bakunin on Anarchy*, 237.

107   Pyotr Kropotkin, "Anarchist Morality" (1890), in *Anarchism: A Collection of Revolutionary Writings*, ed. Roger Baldwin (Mineola: Dover Publications, 2002), 106.

108   Along with Malatesta, several influential anarchists, including Emma Goldman, Alexander Berkman, Rudolf Rocker, and Gustav Landauer, were also explicitly

critical of Kropotkin's engagement in the war; see Paul Avrich, *Anarchist Portraits* (Princeton: Princeton University Press, 1988), 69, 194; Matthew Adams and Ruth Kinna, "Introduction," in *Anarchism, 1914–18: Internationalism, Anti-Militarism and War*, ed. Matthew Adams and Ruth Kinna (Manchester: Manchester University Press, 2017).

109   Pyotr Kropotkin, "The Paris Commune" (1881), in Graham, *Anarchism: A Documentary History of Libertarian Ideas, Vol. 1*, 107.

110   Emma Goldman, "Anarchism: What It Really Stands For," in *Emma Goldman: A Documentary History of the American Years, Vol. 3, Light and Shadows: 1910–1916*, ed. Candace Falk (Stanford: Stanford University Press, 2012), 285, 78.

111   Goldman, *Living My Life*, 402.

112   Goldman, "The Individual, Society and the State," 110.

113   Markus Lundström, "Toward Anarchy: A Historical Sketch of the Anarchism-Democracy Divide," *Theory in Action* 13, no. 1 (January 2020), accessed August 15, 2022, https://doi.org/10.3798/tia.1937-0237.2004.

114   Paul Preston, *The Spanish Civil War: Reaction, Revolution and Revenge* (London: Harper Perennial, 2006), 14; Robert Alexander, *The Anarchists in the Spanish Civil War*, vols. 1–2 (London: Janus, 1999), 1088–89.

115   Paul Preston, "War of Words: The Spanish Civil War and the Historians," in *Revolution and War in Spain 1931–1939*, ed. Paul Preston (London: Routledge, 1993 [1984]), 10.

116   Alexander, *The Anarchists in the Spanish Civil War*, 235–36, 490–91, 679–80.

117   Preston, *The Spanish Civil War*, 246–48.

118   Woodcock, "Democracy, Heretical and Radical," 24.

119   Herbert Read, *Poetry and Anarchism* (New York: Books for Libraries Press, 1938), 92.

120   Gaston Laval, "Collectives in the Spanish Revolution" (1971), in Graham, *Anarchism: A Documentary History of Libertarian Ideas, Vol. 1*, 478, 80.

121   Noam Chomsky, "Intellectuals and the State," in *Towards a New Cold War: Essays on the Current Crisis and How We Got There*, ed. Noam Chomsky (New York: Pantheon Books, 1982 [1978]), 66.

122   Bakunin, "Statism and Anarchy," 336–37.

123   Alexander Berkman, "To the Youth of America" (1917), in *Life of an Anarchist: The Alexander Berkman Reader*, ed. Gene Fellner (New York: Seven Stories Press, 2005), 146.

124   Noam Chomsky, *Deterring Democracy* (London: Verso, 1991), 375.

125   "Democracy Is a Threat to any Power System: Noam Chomsky Interviewed by John Nichols at Tucson Festival of Books," Chomsky.info, accessed August 23, 2022, https://chomsky.info/0313201.

126   Noam Chomsky, "Bill Moyers' Conversation with Noam Chomsky," in *A World of Ideas: Conversations with Thoughtful Men and Women About American Life Today and the Ideas Shaping Our Future*, ed. Bill Moyers (New York: Doubleday Books, 1989), 47, 53.

127   Nettlau, *A Short History of Anarchism*, 187–88.

128   Paul Goodman, "What Must Be the Revolutionary Program?" (1945), in *The Paul Goodman Reader*, ed. Taylor Stoehr (Oakland: PM Press, 2011), 43.

129   Maurice Joyeux, "Self-Management, Syndicalism and Factory Councils" (1973), in *Anarchism: A Documentary History of Libertarian Ideas, Vol. 2, The Emergence*

of the New Anarchism (1939–1977), ed. Robert Graham (Montréal: Black Rose Books, 2009), 247.

130 Murray Bookchin, "The Greening of Politics: Toward a New Kind of Political Practice," *Green Perspectives: Newsletter of the Green Program Project* no. 1 (January 1986): 5.

131 Amedeo Bertolo, "Democracy and Beyond," *Democracy & Nature* 5, no. 2 (1999), accessed August 15, 2022, https://theanarchistlibrary.org/library/amedeo-bertolo-democracy-and-beyond.

132 Graeber's periodization here differs from that of Colin Ward, who associated the anarchist reemergence with the countercultural movement of the late 1960s; see David Graeber, "The New Anarchists," *New Left Review* 13, (January 2002): 61–62, 69; David Graeber, *The Democracy Project: A History, a Crisis, a Movement* (New York: Spiegel & Grau, 2013), 192; "Colin Ward, The Anarchist Contribution" (1970), in Roussopoulos and Benello, *Participatory Democracy*, 255.

133 Cindy Milstein, "Democracy Is Direct," in *Anarchism and Its Aspirations*, ed. Cindy Milstein (Oakland: AK Press, 2010), 101, 07; *emphasis added*.

134 David Graeber, *Direct Action: An Ethnography* (Oakland: AK Press, 2009), 228–37.

135 Murray Bookchin, *The Ecology of Freedom: The Emergence and Dissolution of Hierarchy* (Plano Alto: Cheshire Books, 1982), 339.

136 Uri Gordon, "Democracy: The Patriotic Temptation," CrimethInc., May 26, 2016, accessed August 12, 20922, https://crimethinc.com/2016/05/26/democracy-the-patriotic-temptation.

137 Bookchin, *The Ecology of Freedom*, 336.

138 Murray Bookchin, *Post-Scarcity Anarchism* (Montréal: Black Rose Books, 1986 [1971]), 180, 77–85.

139 Murray Bookchin, "Thoughts on Libertarian Municipalism," *Left Green Perspectives* no. 41 (January 2000), accessed August 15, 2022, http://social-ecology.org/wp/1999/08/thoughts-on-libertarian-municipalism.

140 Murray Bookchin, *Social Anarchism or Lifestyle Anarchism: An Unbridgeable Chasm* (Oakland: AK Press, 1995), 16–19, 56–61.

141 David Graeber was a key figure in this movement, not least as the formulator of the epic Occupy slogan "we are the 99%." See Graeber, *The Democracy Project*, 40–41.

142 Ibid., 192–96, 210–32. It should be noted that Graeber renounced what he reads as Bookchin's eventual embracement of majority rule; ibid., 195.

143 Ibid., 193.

144 Ibid., 186.

145 Ibid., 224–25.

146 Ibid., 211.

147 Ibid., 154.

148 Ibid., 169–70, 87.

149 See, for instance, Ruth Kinna, Alex Prichard, and Thomas Swann, "Occupy and the Constitution of Anarchy," *Global Constitutionalism* 8, no. 2 (2019); Andrew Flood, "Assemblies Are the Revolution" (2011) in *Anarchism: A Documentary History of Libertarian Ideas, Vol. 3, The New Anarchism (1974–2012)*, ed. Robert Graham (Montréal: Black Rose Books, 2013).

150 Eduardo Colombo, *La voluntad del pueblo: Democracia y anarquía* (Buenos Aires: Tupac Ediciones, 2006), 92–93.

151 Eduardo Colombo, "On Voting," in *Anarchism: A Documentary History of Libertarian Ideas, Vol. 3*, 50.

152 George Benello, "We Are Caught in a Wasteland Culture" (1967), in *From the Ground Up: Essays on Grassroots and Workplace Democracy by George Benello*, ed. Len Krimerman, Frank Lindenfeld, Carol Korty, and Julian Benello (Montréal: Black Rose Books, 1992), 27.

153 Dimitrios Roussopoulos and George Benello, "Preface and Introduction," in *Participatory Democracy: Prospects for Democratizing Democracy*, x–xi, 4.

154 Ibid., 8.

155 Sam Dolgoff, *The Relevance of Anarchism to Modern Society* (Tucson: Sharp Press, 2001 [1977]), 13.

156 For a brief introduction to the anarchist sentiments of the Sarvodaya movement, see Ramnath, *Decolonizing Anarchism*, 188–203.

157 Vinoba Bhave, "Sarvodaya: Freedom From Government" (1952), in Graham, *Anarchism: A Documentary History of Libertarian Ideas, Vol. 1*, 183. It should be noted, however, that Jayaprakash Narayan, the most influential Gandhian theorist alongside Bhave, came to advocate what he called "democratic socialism," a type of libertarian socialist state contrasted with the dominant state communism of China and USSR; see Ramnath, *Decolonizing Anarchism*, 195–98.

158 Robert Graham's blog/archive being one important exception; see "Anarchy & Democracy: Bookchin, Malatesta & Fabbri," Robert Graham's Anarchism Weblog, 2012, accessed August 12, 2022, https://robertgraham.wordpress.com/anarchy-democracy-bookchin-malatesta-fabbri.

159 Luce Fabbri, "Respuesta a la revista "A" ¿Defender la democracia?—Aclacación de Luce Fabbri, en carta publicada en la revista no. 98, (Febrero 1982)," in *El anarquismo: Mas alla de la democracia*, ed. Luce Fabbri (Brasil: Editorial Reconstruir, 1983), 36; *author's translation*.

160 Luce Fabbri, "From Democracy to Anarchy" (1983), in "Anarchy & Democracy: Bookchin, Malatesta & Fabbri," ed. Robert Graham, Robert Graham's Anarchism Weblog, accessed August 15, 2022, https://robertgraham.wordpress.com/anarchy-democracy-bookchin-malatesta-fabbri.

161 Ibid.

162 James Scott, *Two Cheers for Anarchism: Six Easy Pieces on Autonomy, Dignity, and Meaningful Work and Play* (Princeton: Princeton University Press, 2012), xvi.

163 Colin Ward, *Anarchy in Action* (London: Freedom Press, 1996 [1973]), 26.

164 Robert Paul Wolff, *In Defense of Anarchism* (Berkeley: University of California Press, 1998 [1970]), 18.

165 Malatesta, "Toward Anarchy" (1899), in Turcato, *The Method of Freedom*, 300.

166 Malatesta, "Article Excerpt From *Pensiero e Volantà*, May 16, 1925," in Richards, *Errico Malatesta*, 23.

167 Malatesta, "The Anarchists in the Present Time" (1930), in Turcato, *The Method of Freedom*, 504; also see Malatesta's defense of gradualism in Malatesta, "Gradualism" (1925), in ibid.

168 Malatesta, "Article Excerpt From *Pensiero e Volantà*, August 1, 1926," in Richards, *Errico Malatesta*, 150.

169 Lucien van der Walt and Michael Schmidt, *Black Flame: The Revolutionary Class Politics of Anarchism & Syndicalism, Counter-Power Vol. 1* (Oakland: AK Press, 2009), 70.

170 It should be noted that Michael Schmidt has become increasingly affiliated with radical nationalism, and this is not, we must remember, the first time influential anarchist thinkers have failed to translate anarchism into feminist and anti-racist stances; Proudhon (in)famously embraced both misogynous and antisemitic sentiments; Bakunin's notion of Pan-Slavism contains distinct nationalist elements. For a critical discussion on this important theme, see Luther Blissett, *Anarchist Integralism: Aesthetics, Politics and the Après-Garde* (London: Sabotage Editions, 1997); Sharif Gemie, "Anarchism and Feminism: A Historical Survey," *Women's History Review* 5, no. 3 (September 1996).

171 CrimethInc. Ex-Workers Collective, *From Democracy to Freedom: The Difference Between Government and Self-Determination* (Salem: CrimethInc. Far East, 2017), 42.

172 Ibid., 36.

173 Ibid., 42.

174 Malatesta, "Neither Democrats, nor Dictators: Anarchists" (1926), in Richards, *The Anarchist Revolution*, 73–74.

175 Provos, "'Provo' Magazine Leaflet" (1965), in Graham, *Anarchism: A Documentary History of Libertarian, Vol. 2*, 283.

176 Peter Gelderloos, "What Is Democracy?" Anarchist Library, 2004, accessed August 12, 2022, https://theanarchistlibrary.org/library/peter-gelderloos-what-is-democracy.

177 Peter Gelderloos, *Worshiping Power: An Anarchist View of Early State Formation* (Oakland: AK Press, 2016), 1, 237. A similar argument is made in James Scott, *Against the Grain: A Deep History of the Earliest States* (New Haven: Yale University Press, 2017).

178 Uri Gordon, *Anarchy Alive! An Anti-Authoritarian Politics from Practice to Theory* (London: Pluto Press, 2008), 70.

179 Gordon, "Democracy."

180 Mick Smith, *Against Ecological Sovereignty: Ethics, Biopolitics, and Saving the Natural World* (Minneapolis: University of Minnesota Press, 2011), xii.

181 Ibid., xiii.

182 Ibid., 77.

183 Henry David Thoreau, "Walking," in *The Natural History Essays*, ed. Henry David Thoreau (Layton: Gibbs Smith, 2011 [1862]), 93.

184 John Zerzan, *Twilight of the Machines* (Los Angeles: Feral House, 2008), viii.

185 Ibid., 24.

186 Ibid., 95.

187 Moxy Marlinspike and Windy Hart, "An Anarchist Critique of Democracy," Anarchist Library, November 1, 2005, accessed August 15, 2022, https://tinyurl.com/52veu525.

188 Anonymous (Corin Bruce), "Green Anarchism: Towards the Abolition of Hierarchy," Anarchist Library, accessed August 15, 2022, https://

theanarchistlibrary.org/library/corin-bruce-green-anarchism-towards-the-abolition-of-hierarchy.

189 Zerzan, *Twilight of the Machines*, 62.

190 Reclus, "On Vegetarianism" (1901), in *Anarchy, Geography, Modernity*, 161.

191 One brief exception being Aragorn Eloff, "Do Anarchists Dream of Emancipated Sheep? Contemporary Anarchism, Animal Liberation and the Implications of New Philosophy," in *Anarchism and Animal Liberation: Essays on Complementary Elements of Total Liberation*, ed. Erika Cudworth, Richard White, and Anthony Nocella (Jefferson: McFarland & Company, 2015), 196–98.

192 See Édith Thomas, *Louise Michel* (Montréal: Black Rose Books, 1980), 96–99, 395–97.

193 Louise Michel, "Memoirs of Louise Michel" (1886), in *The Red Virgin: Memoirs of Louise Michel*, ed. Bullitt Lowry and Elizabeth Gunter (Tuscaloosa: University of Alabama Press, 1981), 24.

194 Ibid., 139.

195 Ibid., 141.

196 Emma Goldman, "Voltairine de Cleyre" (1932), in *Exquisite Rebel: The Essays of Voltairine de Cleyre—Anarchist, Feminist, Genius*, ed. Sharon Presley and Crispin Sartwell (New York: State University of New York Press, 2005), 41–42.

197 Markus Lundström, "'We Do This Because the Market Demands It': Alternative Meat Production and the Speciesist Logic," *Agriculture and Human Values* 36, no. 1 (March 2019), accessed August 15, 2022, https://doi.org/10.1007/s10460-018-09902-1.

198 Bob Torres, *Making a Killing: The Political Economy of Animal Rights* (Oakland: AK Press, 2007), 30, 126.

199 Brian Dominick, "Anarcho-Veganism Revisited: Twenty Years of 'Veganarchy,'" in *Anarchism and Animal Liberation: Essays on Complementary Elements of Total Liberation*, ed. Erika Cudworth, Richard White, and Anthony Nocella (Jefferson: McFarland & Company, 2015), 24.

200 Erika Cudworth, Richard White, and Anthony Nocella, "Introduction: The Intersections of Critical Animal Studies and Anarchist Studies for Total Liberation," ibid., 8.

201 The intersectional theme of critical animal studies has in turn redefined the boundaries of the revolutionary subject. For an explorative report on examples of resistance from animals in captivity, see Colling Sarat, *Animal Resistance in the Global Capitalist Era* (East Lansing: Michigan State University Press, 2021); Jason Hribal, *Fear of the Animal Planet: The Hidden History of Animal Resistance* (Oakland: AK Press, 2010).

202 Dimitrios Roussopoulos, "Introduction: The Participatory Tradition and the Ironies of History," in Roussopoulos and Benello, *Participatory Democracy*, 261.

203 Laurence Davies, "Individual and Community," in *The Palgrave Handbook of Anarchism*, ed. Carl Levy and Matthew Adams (Cham: Palgrave Macmillan, 2018).

204 Shawn P. Wilbur, "Anarchy and Democracy: Examining the Divide," Center for a Stateless Society, June 6, 2017, accessed August 15, 2022, https://c4ss.org/content/49277.

205 Wayne Price, "Democracy, Anarchism, & Freedom," Center for a Stateless Society, June 3, 2017, accessed August 15, 2022, https://c4ss.org/content/49237.

206 For an contextualizing account of Abdullah Öcalan's theory of democratic confederalism (forged with clear reference to Bookchin), see Michael Knapp, Anja Flach, and Ercan Ayboga, *Revolution in Rojava: Democratic Autonomy and Women's Liberation in Syrian Kurdistan* (London: Pluto Press, 2016), 36–46.

207 Gordon, "Democracy."

208 Invisible Committee, "Get Going!" in *The Coming Insurrection*, ed. Invisible Committee, Anarchist Library, 2007, accessed August 15, 2022, https://theanarchistlibrary.org/library/comite-invisible-the-coming-insurrection.

209 Ruth Kinna, *Anarchism: A Beginner's Guide* (Oxford: Oneworld, 2005), 115.

210 CrimethInc. Ex-Workers Collective, *From Democracy to Freedom*, 34–46, 113.

211 "Delo Truda" Group (Makhno, Mett, Arshinov, Valevski, and Linski), "The Organizational Platform of the General Union of Anarchists," Nestormakhno.info, accessed August 23, 2022, http://www.nestormakhno.info/english/newplatform/org_plat.htm.

212 See, for instance, Paul Avrich, "Introduction," in *The Anarchists in the Russian Revolution*, ed. Paul Avrich (London: Thames and Hudson, 1973), 23–28.

213 Gregory Maksimov, "The Soviets of the Workers', Soldiers' and Peasants' Deputies" (1917), in ibid., 103.

214 Gregory Maksimov, *The Program of Anarcho-Syndicalism* (New York: Guillotine Press, 2015 [1927]), 38.

215 See Avrich and Avrich, *Sasha and Emma*, 349–50.

216 Malatesta, "Malatesta's Reply to Nestor Makhno" (1929), in Richards, *The Anarchist Revolution*, 110.

217 Malatesta, "A Project of Anarchist Organization" (1927), in Turcato, *The Method of Freedom*, 488, 490.

218 Voline, "Book 2, Part 1, Chapter 2: Causes and Consequences of the Bolshevik Conception," in *The Unknown Revolution*, ed. Voline (Detroit: Black & Red, 1974 [1947]), 198.

The Impossible Argument

1   For instance, the police have now been allowed to increase camera surveillance and usage of sound detectors in Husby to prevent further outbursts of what they labeled as social unrest; see Länsstyrelsen Stockholm, *Tillstånd till kameraövervakning: Beteckning 2112-24812-2017* 2017-11-10); Kammarätten I Stockholm, *Dom gällande kameraövervakning vid Tenstaplan och Tenstagången i Stockholm: Mål 7392-15* 2016-06-09.

2   Interview no. 6, June 26, 2013, in Husby.

3   See "Preface," Jacques Rancière, *Proletarian Nights: The Workers' Dream in Nineteenth-Century France* (London: Verso, 2012), iv.

4   Chantal Mouffe, *Agonistics: Thinking of the World Politically* (London: Verso, 2013), 118.

5   Ibid., xiv.

6   Errico Malatesta, "Note on Hz's article, 'Science and Anarchy'" (1925), in *The Anarchist Revolution: Polemical Articles 1924–1931*, ed. Vernon Richards (London: Freedom Press, 1995), 52.

7   Errico Malatesta, "Toward Anarchy" (1899), in *The Method of Freedom: An Errico Malatesta Reader*, ed. Davide Turcato (London: AK Press, 2014), 299.

8   Malatesta, "Against the Constituent Assembly as against the Dictatorship" (1930), in ibid, 509.

9   Peter Marshall, *Demanding the Impossible: A History of Anarchism* (London: Harper Perennial, 2008 [1992]).

10   Rancière, *Proletarian Nights*, ix.

11   Paul Goodman, "Freedom and Autonomy" (1972), in *The Paul Goodman Reader*, ed. Taylor Stoehr (Oakland: PM Press, 2011), 31–32.

12   CrimethInc. Ex-Workers Collective, *From Democracy to Freedom: The Difference Between Government and Self-Determination* (Salem: CrimethInc. Far East, 2017), 42.

13   Malatesta, "Democracy and Anarchy" (1924), in *The Anarchist Revolution: Polemical Articles 1924–1931*, ed. Richards (London: Freedom Press, 1995), 79.

14   Ibid., 80.

15   Errico Malatesta, "Anarchism and Socialism: The Parliamentary Socialists' Refrain" (1897), in *The Complete Works of Malatesta, Vol. 3. A Long and Patient Work: The Anarchist Socialism of L'Agitazione, 1897–1898*, ed. Davide Turcato (Oakland: AK Press, 2016), 252.

16   Errico Malatesta, "Article Excerpt From *Umanità Nova*, October 7, 1922," in *Errico Malatesta: His Life and Ideas*, ed. Vernon Richards (London: Freedom Press, 1965), 171.

17   Malatesta, "Article Excerpt From *Umanità Nova*, September 6, 1921," in ibid., 165.

18   Malatesta, "Note on Hz's article, 'Science and Anarchy,'" 38.

19   Malatesta, "An Anarchist Programme" (1899), in Turcato, *The Method of Freedom*, 292.

20   Malatesta, "Revolution in Practice" (1922), in ibid., 421.

21   Cited in Sam Dolgoff, "Introduction," in *Bakunin on Anarchy: Selected Works by the Activist-Founder of World Anarchism*, ed. Sam Dolgoff (London: Routledge, 2013), 10. It should however be noted that Malatesta opposed Bakunin's infamous attempt to impede governmental regrowth through a secret underground organization of exclusively dedicated revolutionaries; Mikhail Bakunin, "The Program of the International Brotherhood" (1869), in Dolgoff, ibid., 148–55. For a critical evaluation of this particular strand in Bakunin's thought, see Marshall, *Demanding the Impossible*, 271–77.

22   Malatesta, "Let's Demolish—and Then?" (1926), in Turcato, *The Method of Freedom*, 478.

23   I here use the quote from James Guillaume's popular biography on Bakunin that circulates in the movement, though Sam Dolgoff's direct translation reads "the passion for destruction is a constructive passion, too!" See James Guillaume, "Michael Bakunin: A Biographical Sketch" (1907), in Dolgoff, *Bakunin on Anarchy*, 24; Mikhail Bakunin, "The Reaction in Germany" (1842), in ibid., 75.

24   Malatesta, "Gradualism" (1925), in Turcato, *The Method of Freedom*, 473.

25   Malatesta, "Let's Demolish—and Then?" 479.

26   Pyotr Kropotkin, "Anarchism: Its Philosophy and Ideal" (1896), in *Anarchism: A Collection of Revolutionary Writings*, ed. Roger Baldwin (Mineola: Dover Publications, 2002), 136.

27 See Dongyoun Hwang, *Anarchism in Korea: Independence, Transnationalism, and the Question of National Development, 1919–1984* (Albany: State University of New York Press, 2017), 23, 95.

28 Shin Chaeho, "Declaration of the Korean Revolution" (1923), in *Anarchism: A Documentary History of Libertarian Ideas. Vol. 1, From Anarchy to Anarchism (300CE to 1939)*, ed. Robert Graham (Montréal: Black Rose Books, 2005), 374–76.

29 Carol Ehrlich, "Socialism, Anarchism and Feminism," in *Reinventing Anarchy, Again*, ed. Howard Ehrlich (Oakland: AK Press, 1996 [1977]), 185.

30 See, for instance, Paul Raekstad and Sofa Saio Gradin, *Prefigurative Politics: Building Tomorrow Today* (Cambridge: Polity, 2020); Luke Yates, "Prefigurative Politics and Social Movement Strategy: The Roles of Prefiguration in the Reproduction, Mobilisation and Coordination of Movements," *Political Studies* 69, no. 4 (November 2021); Benjamin Franks, "Prefiguration," in *Anarchism: A Conceptual Approach*, ed. Benjamin Franks, Nathan Jun, and Leonard Williams (New York: Routledge, 2018).

31 Gustav Landauer, "Weak Statesmen, Weaker People!" (1910), in *Revolution and Other Writings: A Political Reader*, ed. and trans. Gabriel Kuhn (Oakland: PM Press, 2010), 214.

32 As noted in Richard Day, *Gramsci Is Dead: Anarchist Currents in the Newest Social Movements* (London: Pluto Press, 2005), 123–26.

33 As noted in Alexandre Christoyannopoulos and Matthew Adams, "Anarchism and Religion: Mapping an Increasingly Fruitful Landscape," in *Essays in Anarchism and Religion*, vol. 1, ed. Alexandre Christoyannopoulos and Matthew Adams (Stockholm: Stockholm University Press, 2017).

34 Bart De Ligt, *The Conquest of Violence: An Essay on War and Revolution* (London: Pluto Press, 1989 [1937]), 75.

35 It should be noted that Tolstoy—like Godwin, Stirner, Thoreau, and Gandhi—did *not* affiliate himself with the anarchist movement (which he associated with violence). Nevertheless, Tolstoy's was indeed a prominent and influential voice against the notion of government, which has made him imperative for anarchist thought. Following Paul Eltzbacher's list of key anarchist thinkers (1911), Max Nettlau (1932) has located Tolstoy alongside Bakunin and Kropotkin, just as George Woodcock (1962) and Peter Marshall (1992) have recognized Tolstoy's profound contribution to the anarchist tradition.

36 Lev Tolstoy, "On Anarchy" (1900), in *Government Is Violence: Essays on Anarchism and Pacifism*, ed. David Stephens (London: Phoenix Press, 1990), 68.

37 Tolstoy, "Patriotism and Government" (1900), in ibid., 86–87.

38 Tolstoy, "The Slavery of Our Times" (1900), in ibid., 145.

39 Simon Springer, "Public Space as Emancipation: Meditations on Anarchism, Radical Democracy, Neoliberalism and Violence," *Antipode* 43, no. 2 (March 2011): 551, accessed August 15, 2022, https://doi.org/10.1111/j.1467-8330.2010.00827.x.

40 CrimethInc. Ex-Workers Collective, *From Democracy to Freedom*, 72, 75.

41 Jacques Rancière, *Hatred of Democracy* (London: Verso, 2006), 49.

42 Miguel Abensour, *Democracy against the State: Marx and the Machiavellian Moment* (Cambridge: Polity, 2011 [1997]), xxx–xli, 96.

Bibliography

Abensour, Miguel. *Democracy against the State: Marx and the Machiavellian Moment.* Cambridge: Polity, 2011 [1997].

Ackelsberg, Martha. *Free Women of Spain: Anarchism and the Struggle for the Emancipation of Women.* Oakland: AK Press, 2005 [1991].

Adams, Matthew, and Ruth Kinna. "Introduction." In *Anarchism, 1914–18: Internationalism, Anti-militarism and War.* Edited by Matthew Adams and Ruth Kinna, 1–28. Manchester: Manchester University Press, 2017.

Alexander, Robert. *The Anarchists in the Spanish Civil War*, vols. 1–2. London: Janus, 1999.

Amster, Randall, Abraham DeLeon, Luis Fernandez, Anthony Nocella, and Deric Shannon. *Contemporary Anarchist Studies: An Introductory Anthology of Anarchy in the Academy.* London: Routledge, 2009.

Anderson, Benedict. *Under Three Flags: Anarchism and the Anti-Colonial Imagination.* London: Verso, 2005.

Anonymous (Corin Bruce). "Green Anarchism: Towards the Abolition of Hierarchy," Anarchist Library. Accessed August 15, 2022. https://theanarchistlibrary.org/library/corin-bruce-green-anarchism-towards-the-abolition-of-hierarchy.

Armand, Émile. "Mini-Manual of the Anarchist Individualist" (1911). Translated by Paul Sharkey. In *Anarchism: A Documentary History of Libertarian Ideas, Vol. 1, From Anarchy to Anarchism (300CE to 1939).* Edited by Robert Graham, 145–49. Montréal: Black Rose Books, 2005.

Avrich, Paul. *Anarchist Portraits.* Princeton: Princeton University Press, 1988.

———. *The Haymarket Tragedy.* Princeton: Princeton University Press, 1984.

———. "Introduction." In *The Anarchists in the Russian Revolution.* Edited by Paul Avrich, 9–29. London: Thames and Hudson, 1973.

Avrich, Paul, and Karen Avrich. *Sasha and Emma: The Anarchist Odyssey of Alexander Berkman and Emma Goldman.* Cambridge: Harvard University Press, 2012.

Bakunin, Mikhail. "Federalism, Socialism, Anti-Theologism" (1867). Translated by Sam Dolgoff. In *Bakunin on Anarchy: Selected Works by the Activist-Founder of World Anarchism.* Edited by Sam Dolgoff, 102–47. London: Routledge, 2013.

———. "God and the State" (1871). Translated by Sam Dolgoff. In *Bakunin on Anarchy: Selected Works by the Activist-Founder of World Anarchism.* Edited by Sam Dolgoff, 225–42. London: Routledge, 2013.

———. "The Illusion of Universal Suffrage" (1870). In *Democracy: A Reader*. Edited by Ricardo Blaug and John Schwarzmantel, 167–69. New York: Columbia University Press, 2016.

———. "Letter to the Internationalists of the Romagna" (1872). In "Colin Ward: The Anarchist Contribution." *In Participatory Democracy: Prospects for Democratizing Democracy*. Edited by Dimitrios Roussopoulos and George Benello, 247–56. Montréal: Black Rose Books, 2005.

———. "On Representative Government and Universal Suffrage" (1870). Translated by Sam Dolgoff. In *Bakunin on Anarchy: Selected Works by the Activist-Founder of World Anarchism*. Edited by Sam Dolgoff, 218–24. London: Routledge, 2013.

———. "The Program of the Alliance" (1871). Translated by Sam Dolgoff. In *Bakunin on Anarchy: Selected Works by the Activist-Founder of World Anarchism*. Edited by Sam Dolgoff, 242–58. London: Routledge, 2013.

———. "The Program of the International Brotherhood" (1869). In *Bakunin on Anarchy: Selected Works by the Activist-Founder of World Anarchism*. Edited by Sam Dolgoff, 148–55. London: Routledge, 2013.

———. "The Reaction in Germany" (1842). Translated by Sam Dolgoff. In *Bakunin on Anarchy: Selected Works by the Activist-Founder of World Anarchism*. Edited by Sam Dolgoff, 55–57. London: Routledge, 2013.

———. "Revolutionary Catechism" (1866). Translated by Sam Dolgoff. In *Bakunin on Anarchy: Selected Works by the Activist-Founder of World Anarchism*. Edited by Sam Dolgoff, 76–97. London: Routledge, 2013.

———. "Statism and Anarchy" (1873). Translated by Sam Dolgoff. In *Bakunin on Anarchy: Selected Works by the Activist-Founder of World Anarchism*. Edited by Sam Dolgoff, 323–50. London: Routledge, 2013.

———. "What Is the State" (1869). Translated by Paul Sharkey. In *Anarchism: A Documentary History of Libertarian Ideas, Vol. 1, From Anarchy to Anarchism (300CE to 1939)*. Edited by Robert Graham, 86–87. Montréal: Black Rose Books, 2005.

Benello, George. "We Are Caught in a Wasteland Culture" (1967). In *From the Ground Up: Essays on Grassroots and Workplace Democracy by George Benello*. Edited by Len Krimerman, Frank Lindenfeld, Carol Korty, and Julian Benello, 15–30. Montréal: Black Rose Books, 1992.

Benhabib, Seyla. "Introduction: The Democratic Moment and the Problem of Difference." In *Democracy and Difference: Contesting the Boundaries of the Political*. Edited by Seyla Benhabib, 3–18. Princeton: Princeton University Press, 1996.

Berkman, Alexander. "Apropos." *Mother Earth Bulletin*, October 1917. Accessed August 15, 2022. http://dwardmac.pitzer.edu/anarchist_archives/goldman/ME/me.html.

———. "To the Youth of America" (1917). In *Life of an Anarchist: The Alexander Berkman Reader*. Edited by Gene Fellner, 146–47. New York: Seven Stories Press, 2005.

Bertolo, Amedeo. "Democracy and Beyond." *Democracy & Nature* 5, no. 2 (1999): 311–22. Accessed August 15, 2022. http://www.democracynature.org/vol5/bertolo_democracy.htm.

Bhave, Vinoba. "Sarvodaya: Freedom from Government" (1952). In *Anarchism: A Documentary History of Libertarian Ideas, Vol. 1, From Anarchy to Anarchism*

(300CE to 1939). Edited by Robert Graham, 183–86. Montréal: Black Rose Books, 2005.

Blissett, Luther. *Anarchist Integralism: Aesthetics, Politics and the Après-Garde*. London: Sabotage Editions, 1997.

Bookchin, Murray. *The Ecology of Freedom: The Emergence and Dissolution of Hierarchy*. Plano Alto: Cheshire Books, 1982.

———. "The Greening of Politics: Toward a New Kind of Political Practice." *Green Perspectives: Newsletter of the Green Program Project* no. 1 (January 1986).

———. *Post-Scarcity Anarchism*, 2nd ed. Montréal: Black Rose Books, 1986 [1971].

———. *Social Anarchism or Lifestyle Anarchism: An Unbridgeable Chasm*. Oakland: AK Press, 1995.

———. "Thoughts on Libertarian Municipalism." *Left Green Perspectives* 41 (January 2000). Accessed August 15, 2022. http://social-ecology.org/wp/1999/08/thoughts-on-libertarian-municipalism.

Boréus, Kristina. "Husbyhändelserna i nyheter och politisk debatt." In *Bortom kravallerna: Konflikt, tillhörighet och representation i Husby*. Edited by Paulina de los Reyes and Magnus Hörnqvist, 69–100. Stockholm: Stockholmia, 2016.

Boréus, Kristina, and Janne Flyghed. "Poliskultur på kollisionskurs." In *Bortom kravallerna: Konflikt, tillhörighet och representation i Husby*. Edited by Paulina de los Reyes and Magnus Hörnqvist, 133–54. Stockholm: Stockholmia, 2016.

Cafiero, Carlo. "Anarchy and Communism" (1880). Translated by Paul Sharkey. In *No Gods No Masters: An Anthology of Anarchism*. Edited by Daniel Guérin. Oakland: AK Press, 2005.

Campbell, Michelle. "Voltairine de Cleyre and the Anarchist Canon." In *Blasting the Canon*. Edited by Ruth Kinna and Süreyyya Evren, 64–81. New York: Punctum Books, 2013.

Chomsky, Noam. "Bill Moyers' Conversation with Noam Chomsky." In *A World of Ideas: Conversations With Thoughtful Men and Women About American Life Today and the Ideas Shaping Our Future*. Edited by Bill Moyers, 38–58. New York: Doubleday Books, 1989.

———. *Deterring Democracy*. London: Verso, 1991.

———. "Intellectuals and the State" (1978). In *Towards a New Cold War: Essays on the Current Crisis and How We Got There*. Edited by Noam Chomsky, 60–86. New York: Pantheon Books, 1982.

Christoyannopoulos, Alexandre, and Matthew Adams. "Anarchism and Religion: Mapping an Increasingly Fruitful Landscape." In *Essays in Anarchism and Religion*, vol. 1. Edited by Alexandre Christoyannopoulos and Matthew Adams, 1–17. Stockholm: Stockholm University Press, 2017.

Clover, Joshua. *Riot. Strike. Riot: The New Era of Uprisings*. London: Verso, 2016.

Cohn, Jesse. *Underground Passages: Anarchist Resistance Culture, 1848–2011*. Oakland: Ak Press, 2015.

Colombo, Eduardo. *La voluntad del pueblo: Democracia y anarquía*. Buenos Aires: Tupac Ediciones, 2006.

———. "On Voting" (2006). Translated by Paul Sharkey. In *Anarchism: A Documentary History of Libertarian Ideas, Vol. 3, the New Anarchism (1974–2012)*. Edited by Robert Graham, 49–53. Montréal: Black Rose Books, 2013.

CrimethInc. Ex-Workers Collective. *From Democracy to Freedom: The Difference between Government and Self-Determination*. Salem: CrimethInc. Far East, 2017.

Critchley, Simon. "True Democracy: Marx, Political Subjectivity and Anarchic Meta-Politics." In *Radical Democracy: Identity, Citizenship and the State*. Edited by Lars Tønder and Lasse Thomassen, 219–35. Manchester: Manchester University Press, 2005.

Cudworth, Erika, Richard White, and Anthony Nocella. "Introduction: The Intersections of Critical Animal Studies and Anarchist Studies for Total Liberation." In *Anarchism and Animal Liberation: Essays on Complementary Elements of Total Liberation*. Edited by Erika Cudworth, Richard White, and Anthony Nocella, 7–20. Jefferson: McFarland & Company, 2015.

Cutler, Robert. "Introduction." In *Mikhail Bakunin: From Out of the Dustbin, Bakunin's Basic Writings 1869–1871*. Edited by Robert Cutler, 15–29. Ann Arbor: Ardis, 1985.

Dahl, Robert. *On Democracy*. New Haven: Yale University Press, 1998.

Davies, Laurence. "Individual and Community." In *The Palgrave Handbook of Anarchism*. Edited by Carl Levy and Matthew Adams, 47–69. Cham: Palgrave Macmillan, 2018.

Day, Richard. *Gramsci Is Dead: Anarchist Currents in the Newest Social Movements*. London: Pluto Press, 2005.

De Cleyre, Voltairine. "The Making of an Anarchist" (1903). In *The Voltairine de Cleyre Reader*. Edited by A.J. Brigati, 105–11. Oakland: AK Press, 2004.

———. "The Political Equality of Woman" (1894). In *Exquisite Rebel: The Essays of Voltairine De Cleyre: Feminist, Anarchist, Genius*. Edited by Sharon Presley and Crispin Sartwell, 241–43. New York: State University of New York Press, 2005.

De los Reyes, Paulina. "Husby, våldet och talandets villkor." In *Bortom kravallerna: Konflikt, tillhörighet och representation i Husby*. Edited by Paulina de los Reyes and Magnus Hörnqvist, 155–86. Stockholm: Stockholmia, 2016.

De los Reyes, Paulina, and Magnus Hörnqvist. "Introduktion. Konflikt, tillhörighet och representation." In *Bortom kravallerna: Konflikt, tillhörighet och representation i Husby*. Edited by Paulina de los Reyes and Magnus Hörnqvist, 7–24. Stockholm: Stockholmia, 2016.

De Los Reyes, Paulina, and Markus Lundström. "Researching Otherwise? Autoethnographic Notes on the 2013 Stockholm Riots." *Critical Sociology* 47, nos. 7–8 (November 2021): 1159–70. Accessed August 15, 2022. https://doi.org/10.1177/0896920520978482.

Dolgoff, Sam. "Introduction." In *Bakunin on Anarchy*. Edited by Sam Dolgoff, 3–21. London: Routledge, 2013.

———. *The Relevance of Anarchism to Modern Society*. Tucson: Sharp Press, 2001 [1977].

Dominick, Brian. "Anarcho-Veganism Revisited: Twenty Years of 'Veganarchy.'" In *Anarchism and Animal Liberation: Essays on Complementary Elements of Total Liberation*. Edited by Erika Cudworth, Richard White, and Anthony Nocella, 23–39. Jefferson: McFarland & Company, 2015.

Ehrlich, Carol. "Socialism, Anarchism and Feminism" (1977). In *Reinventing Anarchy, Again*. Edited by Howard Ehrlich, 169–88. Oakland: AK Press, 1996.

Eloff, Aragorn. "Do Anarchists Dream of Emancipated Sheep? Contemporary Anarchism, Animal Liberation and the Implications of New Philosophy." In *Anarchism and Animal Liberation: Essays on Complementary Elements of Total*

Liberation. Edited by Erika Cudworth, Richard White, and Anthony Nocella, 194–211. Jefferson: McFarland & Company, 2015.

Eltzbacher, Paul. *Anarchism: Seven Exponents of the Anarchist Philosophy*. London: Freedom Press, 1960 [1911].

Epstein, Barbara. "Radical Democracy and Cultural Politics: What About Class? What About Political Power?" In *Radical Democracy: Identity, Citizenship and the State*. Edited by David Trend, 127–39. London: Routledge, 1995.

Fabbri, Luce. "From Democracy to Anarchy." In *Anarchy & Democracy: Bookchin, Malatesta & Fabbri*. Edited by Robert Graham: Robert Graham's Anarchism Weblog. Accessed June 16, 2017, 2012 [1983].

———. "Respuesta a la revista "A" ¿Defender la democracia?—Aclacación de Luce Fabbri, en carta publicada en la revista N°98, de Febrero 1982." In *El anarquismo: Mas alla de la democracia*. Edited by Luce Fabbri. Brasil: Editorial Reconstruir, 1983.

Fabbri, Luigi. "Fascism: The Preventive Counter-Revolution" (1921). Translated by Paul Sharkey. In *Anarchism: A Documentary History of Libertarian Ideas, Vol. 1, From Anarchy to Anarchism (300CE to 1939)*. Edited by Robert Graham, 408–16. Montréal: Black Rose Books, 2005.

Falk, Candace. "Forging Her Place: An Introduction." In *Emma Goldman: A Documentary History of the American Years, Volume 1: Made for America, 1890–1901*. Edited by Candace Falk, 1–84. Berkeley: University of California Press, 2003.

Ferguson, Kathy. *Emma Goldman: Political Thinking in the Streets*. Lanham: Rowman & Littlefield, 2011.

———. "Why Anarchists Need Stirner." In *Max Stirner*. Edited by Saul Newman, 167–88. Basingstoke: Palgrave Macmillan, 2011.

Finn, Mike. *Debating Anarchism: A History of Action, Ideas and Movements*. London: Bloomsbury, 2021.

Flood, Andrew. "Assemblies Are the Revolution" (2011). Translated by Paul Sharkey. In *Anarchism: A Documentary History of Libertarian Ideas, Vol. 3, The New Anarchism (1974–2012)*. Edited by Robert Graham, 61–63. Montréal: Black Rose Books, 2013.

Franks, Benjamin. "Prefiguration." In *Anarchism: A Conceptual Approach*. Edited by Benjamin Franks, Nathan Jun, and Leonard Williams, 28–43. New York: Routledge, 2018.

Fredricks, Shirley. "Feminism: The Essential Ingredient in Federica Montseny's Anarchist Theory." Translated by Shirley Fredricks. In *European Women on the Left: Socialism, Feminism, and the Problems Faced by Political Women, 1880 to the Present*. Edited by Jane Slaughter and Robert Kern, 125–45. Westport: Greenwood Press, 1981.

Galleani, Luigi. "The End of Anarchism" (1907). In *Anarchism: A Documentary History of Libertarian Ideas, Vol. 1, From Anarchy to Anarchism (300CE to 1939)*. Edited by Robert Graham, 119–24. Montréal: Black Rose Books, 2005.

Gelderloos, Peter. "What Is Democracy?" Anarchist Library, 2004. Accessed August 12, 2022. https://theanarchistlibrary.org/library/peter-gelderloos-what-is-democracy.

———. *Worshiping Power: An Anarchist View of Early State Formation*. Oakland: AK Press, 2016.

Gemie, Sharif. "Anarchism and Feminism: A Historical Survey." *Women's History Review* 5, no. 3 (September 1996): 417–44.

Godwin, William. "Enquiry Concerning Political Justice and Its Influence on Morals and Happiness" (1793). In *Romantic Rationalist: A William Godwin Reader*. Edited by Peter Marshall, 68–70. Oakland: PM Press, 2017.

Goldman, Emma. "Anarchism: What It Really Stands For" (1911). In *Emma Goldman: A Documentary History of the American Years, Volume 1: Made for America, 1890–1901*. Edited by Candace Falk, 273–85. Stanford: Stanford University Press, 2012.

———. "The Individual, Society and the State" (1940). In *Red Emma Speaks*. Edited by Alix Kates Schulman, 78–86. Amherst: Humanity Books, 1998.

———. "Jealousy: Causes and a Possible Cure" (1915). In *Red Emma Speaks*. Edited by Alix Kates Schulman, 214–21. Amherst: Humanity Books, 1998.

———. "The Law's Limit (New York World, 17 October 1893)." In *Emma Goldman: A Documentary History of the American Years, Volume 1: Made for America, 1890–1901*. Edited by Candace Falk, 177–82. Berkeley: University of California Press, 2003.

———. "Letter to Stella Ballantine" (1919). In *Emma Goldman: Political Thinking in the Streets*. Edited by Kathy Ferguson, 257. Lanham: Rowman & Littlefield, 2011.

———. *Living My Life: Two Volumes in One*. New York: Cosimo, 2011 [1931].

———. "Minorities Versus Majorities" (1911). In *Red Emma Speaks*. Edited by Alix Kates Schulman, 78–86. Amherst: Humanity Books, 1998.

———. "Some More Observations (Free Society, 29 April 1900)." In *Emma Goldman: A Documentary History of the American Years, Volume 1: Made for America, 1890–1901*. Edited by Candace Falk, 400–03. Berkeley: University of California Press, 2003.

———. "Voltairine de Cleyre" (1932). In *Exquisite Rebel: The Essays of Voltairine de Cleyre—Anarchist, Feminist, Genius*. Edited by Sharon Presley and Crispin Sartwell, 29–44. New York: SUNY Press, 2005.

———. "Woman Suffrage" (1911). In *Red Emma Speaks*. Edited by Alix Kates Schulman, 190–203. Amherst: Humanity Books, 1998.

Gómez Casas, Juan. *Anarchist Organisation: The History of the F.A.I.* Montréal: Black Rose Books, 1986.

Gonzalez, Alejandro. "Husby, mostånd och gemenskap." In *Bortom kravallerna: Konflikt, tillhörighet och representation i Husby*. Edited by Paulina de los Reyes and Magnus Hörnqvist, 51–68. Stockholm: Stockholmia, 2016.

Goodman, Paul. "Freedom and Autonomy" (1972). In *The Paul Goodman Reader*. Edited by Taylor Stoehr, 31–33. Oakland: PM Press, 2011.

———. "What Must Be the Revolutionary Program?" (1945). In *The Paul Goodman Reader*. Edited by Taylor Stoehr, 41–43. Oakland: PM Press, 2011.

Gordon, Uri. *Anarchy Alive! An Anti-Authoritarian Politics from Practice to Theory*. London: Pluto Press, 2008.

———. "Democracy: The Patriotic Temptation." CrimethInc., May 26, 2016. Accessed August 15, 2022. https://crimethinc.com/2016/05/26/democracy-the-patriotic-temptation.

Gornick, Vivian. *Emma Goldman: Revolution as a Way of Life*. New Haven: Yale University Press, 2011.

Graeber, David. *The Democracy Project: A History, a Crisis, a Movement*. New York: Spiegel & Grau, 2013.

————. *Direct Action: An Ethnography*. Oakland: AK Press, 2009.

————. "The New Anarchists." *New Left Review* 13 (January 2002): 61–73.

Graham, Robert. "Anarchy and Democracy: Bookchin, Malatesta and Fabbri." Robert Graham's Anarchism Weblog, January 13, 2012. Accessed August 16, 2022. https://robertgraham.wordpress.com/anarchy-democracy-bookchin-malatesta-fabbri.

————. "Democracy and Anarchy." Robert Graham's Anarchism Weblog, March 6, 2017. Accessed August 12, 2022. https://robertgraham.wordpress.com/2017/06/03/robert-graham-anarchy-and-democracy.

————. "Preface." In *Anarchism: A Documentary History of Libertarian Ideas, Vol. 1, From Anarchy to Anarchism (300CE to 1939)*. Edited by Robert Graham, xi–xiv. Montréal: Black Rose Books, 2005.

Guillaume, James. "Michael Bakunin: A Biographical Sketch" (1907). Translated by Sam Dolgoff. In *Bakunin on Anarchy: Selected Works by the Activist-Founder of World Anarchism*. Edited by Sam Dolgoff, 22–52. London: Routledge, 2013.

He Zhen. "Problems of Women's Liberation" (1907). Translated by Hsiao-Pei Yen. In *Anarchism: A Documentary History of Libertarian Idea, Vol. 1, From Anarchy to Anarchism (300CE to 1939)*. Edited by Robert Graham, 336–41. Montréal: Black Rose Books, 2005.

Honeywell, Carissa. *Anarchism*. Cambridge: Polity, 2021.

Hörnqvist, Magnus. "Riots in the Welfare State: The Contours of a Modern-Day Moral Economy." *European Journal of Criminology* 13, no. 5 (September 2016): 573–89.

Interview no. 1, June 20, 2013, in Husby.

Interview no. 2, June 26, 2013, in Husby.

Interview no. 3, June 12, 2013, in Husby.

Interview no. 6, June 26, 2013, in Husby.

Interview no. 7, June 20, 2013, in Husby.

Interview no. 11, June 20, 2013, in Husby.

Interview no. 13, July 1, 2013, in Kista.

Interview no. 18, June 24, 2013, in Husby.

Interview no. 26, August 7, 2013, in Husby.

Interview no. 29, August 7, 2013, in Husby.

Hribal, Jason. *Fear of the Animal Planet: The Hidden History of Animal Resistance*. Oakland: AK Press, 2010.

Hwang, Dongyoun. *Anarchism in Korea: Independence, Transnationalism, and the Question of National Development, 1919–1984*. Albany: State University of New York Press, 2017.

Invisible Committee. "Get Going!" In *The Coming Insurrection*. Anarchist Library, 2007. Edited by Invisible Committee. Accessed August 15, 2022. https://theanarchistlibrary.org/library/comite-invisible-the-coming-insurrection.

Janicka, Iwona. *Theorizing Contemporary Anarchism: Solidarity, Mimesis and Radical Social Change*. London: Bloomsbury, 2017.

"The Järva Vision" (2016). Accessed September 26, 2016. Unavailable August 11, 2022. http://bygg.stockholm.se/Alla-projekt/Jarvalyftet/In-English.

Joyeux, Maurice "Self-Management, Syndicalism and Factory Councils" (1973). Translated by Paul Sharkey. In *Anarchism: A Documentary History of Libertarian Ideas, Vol. 2, The Emergence of the New Anarchism (1939–1977)*. Edited by Robert Graham, 342–51. Montréal: Black Rose Books, 2009.

Kammarätten i Stockholm. *Dom gällande kameraövervakning vid Tenstaplan och Tenstagången i Stockholm: Mål 7392-15,* June 9, 2016.

Kanno Sugako. "Kanno Sugako" (1911). In *Reflections on the Way to the Gallows: Rebel Women in Prewar Japan.* Edited by Mikiso Hane, 51–74. Berkeley: University of California Press, 1988.

Kinna, Ruth. *Anarchism: A Beginner's Guide.* Oxford: Oneworld, 2005.

———. *The Government of No One: The Theory and Practice of Anarchism.* London: Pelican, 2019.

Kinna, Ruth, Alex Prichard, and Thomas Swann. "Occupy and the Constitution of Anarchy." *Global Constitutionalism* 8, no. 2 (June 2019): 357–90.

Kinna, Ruth, and Süreyyya Evren. *Blasting the Canon.* New York: Punctum Books, 2013.

Knapp, Michael, Anja Flach, Ercan Ayboğa, David Graeber, Asya Abdullah, and Janet Biehl. *Revolution in Rojava: Democratic Autonomy and Women's Liberation in Syrian Kurdistan.* London: Pluto Press, 2016.

Kropotkin, Pyotr. "Anarchism: Its Philosophy and Ideal" (1896). In *Anarchism: A Collection of Revolutionary Writings.* Edited by Roger Baldwin, 115–44. Mineola: Dover Publications, 2002.

———. "Anarchist Morality" (1890). In *Anarchism: A Collection of Revolutionary Writings.* Edited by Roger Baldwin, 79–113. Mineola: Dover Publications, 2002.

———. *Modern Science and Anarchism.* London: Freedom Press, 1912.

———. "The Paris Commune" (1881). Translated by Nicolas Walter. In *Anarchism: A Documentary History of Libertarian Ideas, Vol. 1, From Anarchy to Anarchism (300CE to 1939).* Edited by Robert Graham, 107–8. Montréal: Black Rose Books, 2005.

Laclau, Ernesto. "The Future of Radical Democracy." In *Radical Democracy: Identity, Citizenship and the State.* Edited by Lars Tønder and Lasse Thomassen, 256–62. Manchester: Manchester University Press, 2005.

———. *On Populist Reason.* London: Verso, 2005.

Laclau, Ernesto, and Chantal Mouffe. *Hegemony and Socialist Strategy: Towards a Radical Democratic Politics.* London: Verso, 2001 [1985].

Landauer, Gustav. "Weak Statesmen, Weaker People!" (1910). In *Revolution and Other Writings: A Political Reader.* Edited and Translated by Gabriel Kuhn, 213–14. Oakland: PM Press, 2010.

Länsstyrelsen Stockholm. *Tillstånd till kameraövervakning: Beteckning 2112-24812-2017,* October 11, 2017.

Lauri, Marcus. "Vad är problemet med Husby?" In *Bortom kravallerna: Konflikt, tillhörighet och representation i Husby.* Edited by Paulina de los Reyes and Magnus Hörnqvist, 101–32. Stockholm: Stockholmia, 2016.

Laval, Gaston. "Collectives in the Spanish Revolution" (1971). In *Anarchism: A Documentary History of Libertarian Ideas, Vol. 1, From Anarchy to Anarchism (300CE to 1939).* Edited by Robert Graham, 477–82. Montréal: Black Rose Books, 2005.

Leopold, David. "A Solitary Life." In *Max Stirner.* Edited by Saul Newman, 21–41. Basingstoke: Palgrave Macmillan, 2011.

Lewis, Paul, Tim Newburn, Matthew Taylor, Catriona McGillivray, Aster Greenhill, Harold Frayman, and Rob Proctor. *Reading the Riots: Investigating England's*

Summer of Disorder. London: Guardian/LSE, 2011. Accessed August 15, 2022. http://eprints.lse.ac.uk/id/eprint/46297.

Ligt, Bart de. *The Conquest of Violence: An Essay on War and Revolution*. London: Pluto Press, 1989 [1937].

Little, Adrian, and Moya Lloyd. "Introduction." In *The Politics of Radical Democracy*. Edited by Adrian Little and Moya Lloyd, 1–12. Edinburgh: Edinburgh University Press, 2009.

Lloyd, Moya. "Performing Radical Democracy." In *The Politics of Radical Democracy*. Edited by Adrian Little and Moya Lloyd, 33–51. Edinburgh: Edinburgh University Press, 2009.

Lummis, Douglas. *Radical Democracy*. Ithaca: Cornell University Press, 1996.

Lundström, Markus. "'The Ballot Humbug': Anarchist Women and Women's Suffrage." *Moving the Social: Journal of Social History and the History of Social Movements* 66 (2022).

———. "Det demokratiska hotet." In *Bortom kravallerna: Konflikt, tillhörighet och representation i Husby*. Edited by Paulina de los Reyes and Magnus Hörnqvist, 25–50. Stockholm: Stockholmia, 2016.

———. "Toward Anarchy: A Historical Sketch of the Anarchism-Democracy Divide." *Theory in Action* 13, no. 1 (January 2020): 80–114. Accessed August 15, 2022. https://doi.org/10.3798/tia.1937-0237.2004.

———. "'We Do This Because the Market Demands It': Alternative Meat Production and the Speciesist Logic." *Agriculture and Human Values* 36, no. 1 (December 2019): 127–36. Accessed August 15, 2022. https://doi.org/10.1007/s10460-018-09902-1.

Maeckelbergh, Marianne. *The Will of the Many: How the Alterglobalisation Movement Is Changing the Face of Democracy*. London: Pluto Press, 2009.

Maksimov, Gregory. *The Program of Anarcho-Syndicalism*. New York: Guillotine Press, 2015 [1927].

———. "The Soviets of the Workers', Soldiers' and Peasants' Deputies"(1917). In *The Anarchists in the Russian Revolution*. Edited and Translated by Paul Avrich, 102–06. London: Thames and Hudson, 1973.

Malatesta, Errico. "Against the Constituent Assembly as against the Dictatorship" (1930). Translated by Vernon Richards. In *The Method of Freedom: An Errico Malatesta Reader*. Edited by Davide Turcato, 507–10. Oakland: AK Press, 2014.

———. "Anarchism and Reforms" (1924). Translated by Gillian Fleming. In *The Anarchist Revolution: Polemical Articles 1924–1931*. Edited by Vernon Richards, 80–81. London: Freedom Press, 1995.

———. "Anarchism and Socialism: The Parliamentary Socialists' Refrain" (1897). Translated by Paul Sharkey. In *The Complete Works of Malatesta, Vol. 3, A Long and Patient Work: The Anarchist Socialism of L'Agitazione, 1897–1898*. Edited by Davide Turcato, 251–53. Oakland: AK Press, 2016.

———. "An Anarchist Programme" (1899). Translated by Vernon Richards. In *The Method of Freedom: An Errico Malatesta Reader*. Edited by Davide Turcato, 279–93. Oakland: AK Press, 2014.

———. "The Anarchists in the Present Time" (1930). Translated by Paul Sharkey. In *The Method of Freedom: An Errico Malatesta Reader*. Edited by Davide Turcato, 501–06. Oakland: AK Press, 2014.

———. "Anarchy" (1891). Translated by Paul Sharkey. In *The Method of Freedom: An Errico Malatesta Reader*. Edited by Davide Turcato, 109–48. Oakland: AK Press, 2014.

———. "Article Excerpt from *Pensiero e Volantà*, May 16, 1925." In *Errico Malatesta: His Life and Ideas*. Edited by Vernon Richards, 23. London: Freedom Press, 1965.

———. "Article Excerpt from *Pensiero e Volantà*, August 1, 1926." In *Errico Malatesta: His Life and Ideas*. Edited by Vernon Richards, 150–51. London: Freedom Press, 1965.

———. "Article Excerpt from *Umanità Nova*, July 25, 1920." In *Errico Malatesta: His Life and Ideas*. Edited by Vernon Richards, 26. London: Freedom Press, 1965.

———. "Article Excerpt from *Umanità Nova*, September 6, 1921." In *Errico Malatesta: His Life and Ideas*. Edited by Vernon Richards, 165. London: Freedom Press, 1965.

———. "Article Excerpt from *Umanità Nova*, October 6, 1921." In *Errico Malatesta: His Life and Ideas*. Edited by Vernon Richards, 73. London: Freedom Press, 1965.

———. "Article Excerpt from *Umanità Nova*, October 7, 1922." In *Errico Malatesta: His Life and Ideas*. Edited by Vernon Richards, 171–72. London: Freedom Press, 1965.

———. "Collectivism, Communism, Socialist Democracy and Anarchism" (1897). Translated by Paul Sharkey. In *The Complete Works of Malatesta, Vol. 3, A Long and Patient Work: The Anarchist Socialism of L'Agitazione, 1897–1898*. Edited by Davide Turcato, 234–37. Oakland: AK Press, 2016.

———. "Communism and Individualism (Comment on an Article by Max Nettlau)" (1926). Translated by Gillian Fleming. In *The Anarchist Revolution: Polemical Articles 1924–1931*. Edited by Vernon Richards, 13–18. London: Freedom Press, 1995.

———. "Democracy and Anarchy" (1924). Translated by Gillian Fleming. In *The Anarchist Revolution: Polemical Articles 1924–1931*. Edited by Vernon Richards, 76–79. London: Freedom Press, 1995.

———. "From a Matter of Tactics to a Matter of Principle" (1897). Translated by Paul Sharkey. In *The Method of Freedom: An Errico Malatesta Reader*. Edited by Davide Turcato, 413–17. Oakland: AK Press, 2014.

———. "Gradualism" (1925). Translated by Paul Sharkey. In *The Method of Freedom: An Errico Malatesta Reader*. Edited by Davide Turcato, 469–74. Oakland: AK Press, 2014.

———. "Individualism and Anarchism" (1924). Translated by Paul Sharkey. In *The Method of Freedom: An Errico Malatesta Reader*. Edited by Davide Turcato, 459–62. Oakland: AK Press, 2014.

———. "Individualism in Anarchism" (1897). Translated by Paul Sharkey. In *The Complete Works of Malatesta, Vol. 3, A Long and Patient Work: The Anarchist Socialism of L'Agitazione, 1897–1898*. Edited by Davide Turcato, 77–81. Oakland: AK Press, 2016.

———. "Let's Demolish—and Then?" (1926). Translated by Paul Sharkey. In *The Method of Freedom: An Errico Malatesta Reader*. Edited by Davide Turcato, 475–79. Oakland: AK Press, 2014.

———. "Malatesta's Reply to Nestor Makhno" (1929). Translated by Gillian Fleming. In *The Anarchist Revolution: Polemical Articles 1924–1931*. Edited by Vernon Richards, 106–11. London: Freedom Press, 1995.

———. "Neither Democrats, nor Dictators: Anarchists" (1926). Translated by Gillian Fleming. In *The Anarchist Revolution: Polemical Articles 1924–1931.* Edited by Vernon Richards, 73–76. London: Freedom Press, 1995.

———. "Note on Hz's article, 'Science and Anarchy'" (1925). Translated by Gillian Fleming. In *The Anarchist Revolution: Polemical Articles 1924–1931.* Edited by Vernon Richards, 49–52. London: Freedom Press, 1995.

———. "Our Plans: Union Between Communists and Collectivists" (1899). Translated by Paul Sharkey. In *The Method of Freedom: An Errico Malatesta Reader.* Edited by Davide Turcato, 95–99. Oakland: AK Press, 2014.

———. "A Project of Anarchist Organization" (1927). Translated by Vernon Richards. In *The Method of Freedom: An Errico Malatesta Reader.* Edited by Davide Turcato, 481–91. Oakland: AK Press, 2014.

———. "Republic and Revolution" (1924). Translated by Gillian Fleming. In *The Anarchist Revolution: Polemical Articles 1924–1931.* Edited by Vernon Richards, 34–38. London: Freedom Press, 1995.

———. "Revolution in Practice" (1922). Translated by Paul Sharkey. In *The Method of Freedom: An Errico Malatesta Reader.* Edited by Davide Turcato, 419–22. Oakland: AK Press, 2014.

———. "The Socialists and the Elections: A Letter From E. Malatesta" (1897). Translated by Paul Sharkey. In *The Method of Freedom: An Errico Malatesta Reader.* Edited by Davide Turcato, 209–11. Oakland: AK Press, 2014.

———. "Toward Anarchy" (1899). Translated by Paul Sharkey. In *The Method of Freedom: An Errico Malatesta Reader.* Edited by Davide Turcato, 299–302. Oakland: AK Press, 2014.

———. "Violence as a Social Factor" (1895). In *Anarchism: A Documentary History of Libertarian Ideas, Vol. 1, From Anarchy to Anarchism (300CE to 1939).* Edited by Robert Graham, 160–63. Montréal: Black Rose Books, 2005.

Marlinspike, Moxie, and Windy Hart. "An Anarchist Critique of Democracy," Anarchist Library, November 1, 2005. Accessed August 15, 2022. https://tinyurl.com/52veu525.

Marshall, Peter. *Demanding the Impossible: A History of Anarchism.* London: Harper Perennial, 2008 [1992].

Michel, Louise. "Memoirs of Louise Michel" (1886). In *The Red Virgin: Memoirs of Louise Michel.* Edited by Bullitt Lowry and Elizabeth Gunter, 1–197. Tuscaloosa: University of Alabama Press, 1981.

Milstein, Cindy. "Democracy Is Direct." In *Anarchism and Its Aspirations.* Edited by Cindy Milstein, 97–107. Oakland: AK Press, 2010.

Mouffe, Chantal. *Agonistics: Thinking of the World Politically.* London: Verso, 2013.

———. "Preface: Democratic Politics Today." In *Dimensions of Radical Democracy: Pluralism, Citizenship, Community.* Edited by Chantal Mouffe, 1–14. London: Verso, 1992.

Nettlau, Max. *A Short History of Anarchism.* Edited by Heiner Becker. London: Freedom Press, 2000 [1932].

Newman, Saul. "Introduction: Re-encountering Stirner's Ghosts." In *Max Stirner.* Edited by Saul Newman, 1–18. Basingstoke: Palgrave Macmillan, 2011.

———. *Postanarchism.* Cambridge: Polity Press, 2016.

Norval, Aletta. "Radical Democracy." In *Encyclopedia of Democratic Thought.* Edited by Paul Barry Clarke and Joe Foweraker, 587–94. New York: Routledge, 2001.

Pakieser, Andrea. *I Belong Only to Myself: The Life and Writings of Leda Rafanelli.* Oakland: AK Press, 2014.

Parsons, Lucy. "The Ballot Humbug. A Delusion and a Snare; a Mere Veil Behind which Politics Is Played" (1905). In *Lucy Parsons: Freedom, Equality & Solidarity: Writings & Speeches, 1878–1937.* Edited by Roxanne Dunbar-Ortiz, 95–97. Chicago: Charles H. Kerr, 2004.

Presley, Sharon, and Crispin Sartwell. *Exquisite Rebel: The Essays of Voltairine de Cleyre—Anarchist, Feminist, Genius.* New York: State University of New York Press, 2005.

Preston, Paul. *The Spanish Civil War: Reaction, Revolution and Revenge.* London: Harper Perennial, 2006.

———. "War of Words: The Spanish Civil War and the Historians" (1894). In *Revolution and War in Spain 1931–1939.* Edited by Paul Preston. London: Routledge, 1993.

Price, Wayne. "Democracy, Anarchism, & Freedom." Center for Stateless Society, June 3, 2017. Accessed August 15, 2022. https://c4ss.org/content/49237.

Proudhon, Pierre-Joseph. *General Idea of the Revolution in the Nineteenth Century.* New York: Haskell House Publishers, 1969 [1851].

———. *What Is Property? An Inquiry Into the Principle of Right and of Government.* New York: Dover Publications, 1970 [1840].

Provos, "'Provo' Magazine Leaflet" (1965). In *Anarchism: A Documentary History of Libertarian Ideas, Vol. 2, The Emergence of the New Anarchism (1939–1977).* Edited by Robert Graham, 282–88. Montréal: Black Rose Books, 2009.

Putnam, Robert, Robert Leonardi, and Raffaella Nanetti. *Making Democracy Work: Civic Traditions in Modern Italy.* Princeton: Princeton University Press, 1993.

Raekstad, Paul, and Sofa Saio Gradin. *Prefigurative Politics: Building Tomorrow Today.* Cambridge: Polity, 2020.

Ramnath, Maia. *Decolonizing Anarchism: An Antiauthoritarian History of India's Liberation Struggle.* Oakland: AK Press, 2011.

Rancière, Jacques. *Hatred of Democracy.* London: Verso, 2006.

———. *Proletarian Nights: The Workers' Dream in Nineteenth-Century France.* London: Verso, 2012.

Read, Herbert. *Poetry and Anarchism.* New York: Books for Libraries Press, 1938.

Reclus, Élisée. "Anarchy" (1894). In *Anarchy, Geography, Modernity: Selected Writings of Elisée Reclus.* Edited by John Clark and Camille Martin, 120–31. Oakland: PM Press, 2013.

———. "The Modern State" (1905). In *Anarchy, Geography, Modernity: Selected Writings of Elisée Reclus.* Edited by John Clark and Camille Martin, 186–201. Oakland: PM Press, 2013.

———. "On Vegetarianism" (1901). In *Anarchy, Geography, Modernity: Selected Writings of Elisée Reclus.* Edited by John Clark and Camille Martin, 156–62. Oakland: PM Press, 2013.

Richards, Vernon. "Notes for a Biography." In *Errico Malatesta: His Life and Ideas.* Edited by Vernon Richards, 201–42. London: Freedom Press, 1965.

Roussopoulos, Dimitrios. "Introduction: The Participatory Tradition and the Ironies of History." In *Participatory Democracy: Prospects for Democratizing Democracy.* Edited by Dimitrios Roussopoulos and George Benello, 259–69. Montréal: Black Rose Books, 2005.

Roussopoulos, Dimitrios, and George Benello. "Preface and Introduction." In *Participatory Democracy: Prospects for Democratizing Democracy*. Edited by Dimitrios Roussopoulos and George Benello, x–10. Montréal: Black Rose Books, 2005.

Sarat, Colling. *Animal Resistance in the Global Capitalist Era*. East Lansing: Michigan State University Press, 2021.

Schierup, Carl-Ulrik, Aleksandra Ålund, and Lisa Kings. "Reading the Stockholm Riots: A Moment for Social Justice?" *Race & Class* 55, no. 3 (January 2014): 1–21.

Schippers, Birgit. "Judith Butler, Radical Democracy and Micro-Politics." In *The Politics of Radical Democracy*. Edited by Adrian Little and Moya Lloyd, 73–92. Edinburgh: Edinburgh University Press, 2009.

Schumpeter, Joseph. *Capitalism, Socialism and Democracy*. New York: Routledge, 2005 [1943].

Scott, James. *Against the Grain: A Deep History of the Earliest States*. New Haven: Yale University Press, 2017.

———. *Two Cheers for Anarchism: Six Easy Pieces on Autonomy, Dignity, and Meaningful Work and Play*. Princeton: Princeton University Press, 2012.

Sernhede, Ove, Catharina Thörn, and Håkan Thörn. "The Stockholm Uprising in Context: Urban Social Movements in the Rise and Demise of the Swedish Welfare-State City." In *Urban Uprisings: Challenging Neoliberal Urbanism in Europe*. Edited by Margit Mayer, Catharina Thörn, and Håkan Thörn, 149–73. London: Palgrave Macmillan, 2016.

Shin Chaeho. "Declaration of the Korean Revolution" (1923). Translated by Dongyoun Hwang. In *Anarchism: A Documentary History of Libertarian Ideas. Vol. 1, From Anarchy to Anarchism (300CE to 1939)*. Edited by Robert Graham, 373–79. Montréal: Black Rose Books, 2005.

Smith, Anna Marie. *Laclau and Mouffe: The Radical Democratic Imaginary*. London: Routledge, 1998.

Smith, Graham. *Democratic Innovations: Designing Institutions for Citizen Participation*. Cambridge: Cambridge University Press, 2009.

Smith, Mick. *Against Ecological Sovereignty: Ethics, Biopolitics, and Saving the Natural World*. Minneapolis: University of Minnesota Press, 2011.

Sousa Santos, Boaventura de, and Leonardo Avritzer. "Introduction: Opening up the Canon of Democracy." In *Democratizing Democracy: Beyond the Liberal Democratic Canon*. Edited by Boaventura de Sousa Santos, xxxiv–lxxiv. London: Verso, 2005.

Springer, Simon. "Public Space as Emancipation: Meditations on Anarchism, Radical Democracy, Neoliberalism and Violence." *Antipode* 43, no. 2 (2011): 525–62. Accessed August 15, 2022. https://doi.org/10.1111/j.1467-8330.2010.00827.x.

Stirner, Max. *The Ego and Its Own*. Edited by David Leopold. Cambridge: Cambridge University Press, 1995 [1870].

Termes, Josep. *Anarquismo y sindicalismo en España: La Primera Internacional (1864–1881)*. Barcelona: Crítica, 2000 [1977].

Thomas, Édith. *Louise Michel*. Montréal: Black Rose Books, 1980.

Thoreau, Henry David. "Walking." In *The Natural History Essays*. Edited by Henry David Thoreau, 93–136. Layton: Gibbs Smith, 2011 [1862].

Tolstoy, Lev. "On Anarchy" (1900). In *Government Is Violence: Essays on Anarchism and Pacifism*. Edited by David Stephens, 68–70. London: Phoenix Press, 1990.

———. "Patriotism and Government" (1900). In *Government Is Violence: Essays on Anarchism and Pacifism*. Edited by David Stephens, 78–92. London: Phoenix Press, 1990.

———. "The Slavery of Our Times" (1900). In *Government Is Violence: Essays on Anarchism and Pacifism*. Edited by David Stephens, 112–55. London: Phoenix Press, 1990.

Tønder, Lars, and Lasse Thomassen. "Introduction: Rethinking Radical Democracy between Abundance and Lack." In *Radical Democracy: Identity, Citizenship and the State*. Edited by Lars Tønder and Lasse Thomassen, 1–13. Manchester: Manchester University Press, 2005.

Torres, Bob. *Making a Killing: The Political Economy of Animal Rights*. Oakland: AK Press, 2007.

Trend, David. "Democracy's Crisis of Meaning." In *Radical Democracy: Identity, Citizenship and the State*. Edited by David Trend, 7–18. London: Routledge, 1995.

———. "Introduction." In *Radical Democracy: Identity, Citizenship and the State*. Edited by David Trend, 1–4. London: Routledge, 1995.

van der Walt, Lucien, and Michael Schmidt. *Black Flame: The Revolutionary Class Politics of Anarchism & Syndicalism: Counter-Power*, vol. 1. Oakland: AK Press, 2009.

Voline. "Book 2, Part 1, Chapter 2: Causes and Consequences of the Bolshevik Conception." In *The Unknown Revolution*. Edited by Voline, 181–206. Detroit: Black & Red, 1974 [1947].

Ward, Colin. "The Anarchist Contribution" (1970). In *Participatory Democracy: Prospects for Democratizing Democracy*. Edited by Dimitrios Roussopoulos and George Benello, 247–56. Montréal: Black Rose Books, 2005.

———. *Anarchy in Action*. London: Freedom Press, 1996 [1973].

Weiss, Penny, and Loretta Kensinger. *Feminist Interpretations of Emma Goldman*. Pennsylvania: Penn State Press, 2007.

Wilbur, Shawn P. "Anarchy and Democracy: Examining the Divide." Center for a Stateless Society, June 6, 2017. Accessed August 15, 2022. https://c4ss.org/content/49277.

Wilson, Charlotte. "Anarchism" (1886). In *Quiet Rumours: An Anarcha-Feminist Reader*, 3rd ed. Edited by Dark Star Collective, 90–91. Oakland: AK Press, 2012.

———. "The Principles and Aims of Anarchists" (1886). In *Quiet Rumours: An Anarcha-Feminist Reader*, 3rd ed. Edited by Dark Star Collective, 91–92. Oakland: AK Press, 2012.

———. "Social Democracy and Anarchism" (1886). In *Quiet Rumours: An Anarcha-Feminist Reader*, 3rd ed. Edited by Dark Star Collective, 83–87. Oakland: AK Press, 2012.

Wolff, Robert Paul. *In Defense of Anarchism*. Berkeley: University of California Press, 1998 [1970].

Woodcock, George. *Anarchism: A History of Libertarian Ideas and Movements*. Cleveland: World Publishing Company, 1962.

———. "Democracy, Heretical and Radical" (1970). In *Participatory Democracy: Prospects for Democratizing Democracy*. Edited by Dimitrios Roussopoulos and George Benello, 11–24. Montréal: Black Rose Books, 2005.

———. *Pierre-Joseph Proudhon: A Biography*. Montréal: Black Rose Books, 1987 [1956].

Yates, Luke. "Prefigurative Politics and Social Movement Strategy: The Roles of Prefiguration in the Reproduction, Mobilisation and Coordination of Movements." *Political Studies* 69, no. 4 (November 2021): 1033–52.

Zarrow, Peter. *Anarchism and Chinese Political Culture.* New York: Columbia University Press, 1990.

———. "He Zhen and Anarcho-Feminism in China." *Journal of Asian Studies* 47, no. 4 (November 1988): 796–813.

Zerzan, John. *Twilight of the Machines.* Los Angeles: Feral House, 2008.

Index

"Passim" (literally "scattered") indicates intermittent discussion of a topic over a cluster of pages.

About the Author

Markus Lundström is a political sociologist focused on anarchist, fascist, and social movement studies. He is the author of *The Making of Resistance: Brazil's Landless Movement and Narrative Enactment* (Springer, 2017) and coeditor of *Nordic Fascism: Fragments of an Entangled History* (Routledge, 2022).

ABOUT PM PRESS

PM Press is an independent, radical publisher of books and media to educate, entertain, and inspire. Founded in 2007 by a small group of people with decades of publishing, media, and organizing experience, PM Press amplifies the voices of radical authors, artists, and activists. Our aim is to deliver bold political ideas and vital stories to all walks of life and arm the dreamers to demand the impossible. We have sold millions of copies of our books, most often one at a time, face to face. We're old enough to know what we're doing and young enough to know what's at stake. Join us to create a better world.

PM Press
PO Box 23912
Oakland, CA 94623
www.pmpress.org

PM Press in Europe
europe@pmpress.org
www.pmpress.org.uk

FRIENDS OF PM PRESS

These are indisputably momentous times—the financial system is melting down globally and the Empire is stumbling. Now more than ever there is a vital need for radical ideas.

In the many years since its founding—and on a mere shoestring—PM Press has risen to the formidable challenge of publishing and distributing knowledge and entertainment for the struggles ahead. With hundreds of releases to date, we have published an impressive and stimulating array of literature, art, music, politics, and culture. Using every available medium, we've succeeded in connecting those hungry for ideas and information to those putting them into practice.

Friends of PM allows you to directly help impact, amplify, and revitalize the discourse and actions of radical writers, filmmakers, and artists. It provides us with a stable foundation from which we can build upon our early successes and provides a much-needed subsidy for the materials that can't necessarily pay their own way. You can help make that happen—and receive every new title automatically delivered to your door once a month—by joining as a Friend of PM Press. And, we'll throw in a free T-shirt when you sign up.

Here are your options:

- **$30 a month** Get all books and pamphlets plus 50% discount on all webstore purchases

- **$40 a month** Get all PM Press releases (including CDs and DVDs) plus 50% discount on all webstore purchases

- **$100 a month** Superstar—Everything plus PM merchandise, free downloads, and 50% discount on all webstore purchases

For those who can't afford $30 or more a month, we have **Sustainer Rates** at $15, $10, and $5. Sustainers get a free PM Press T-shirt and a 50% discount on all purchases from our website.

Your Visa or Mastercard will be billed once a month, until you tell us to stop. Or until our efforts succeed in bringing the revolution around. Or the financial meltdown of Capital makes plastic redundant. Whichever comes first.

The George Floyd Uprising

Edited by Vortex Group

ISBN: 978-1-62963-966-6
$22.95   288 pages

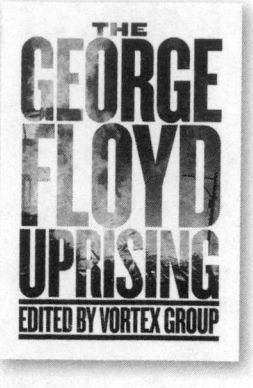

In the summer of 2020, America experienced one of the biggest uprisings in half a century. Waves of enraged citizens took to the streets to streets in Minneapolis to decry the murder of George Floyd at the hands of the police. Battles broke out night after night, with a pandemic weary populace fighting the police and eventually burning down the Third Precinct. The revolt soon spread to cities large and small across the country where protesters set police cars on fire, looted luxury shopping districts and forced the president into hiding in a bunker beneath the White House. As the initial crest receded, localized rebellions continued to erupt throughout the summer and into the fall in Atlanta, Chicago, Kenosha, Louisville, Philadelphia, and elsewhere.

Written during the riots, *The George Floyd Uprising* is a compendium of the most radical writing to come out of that long, hot summer. These incendiary dispatches—from those on the frontlines of the struggle—examines the revolt and the obstacles it confronted. It paints a picture of abolition in practice, discusses how the presence of weapons in the uprising and the threat of armed struggle play out in an American context, and shows how the state responds to and pacifies rebellions. *The George Floyd Uprising* poses new social, tactical, and strategic plans for those actively seeking to expand and intensify revolts of the future. This practical, inspiring collection is essential reading for all those hard at work toppling the state and creating a new revolutionary tradition.

"Exemplary reflections from today's frontline warriors that will disconcert liberals but inspire young people who want to live the struggle in the revolutionary tradition of Robert F. Williams, the Watts 65 rebels, and Deacons for Defense and Justice."
—Mike Davis, author of *Planet of Slums* and *Old Gods, New Enigmas*

"This anthology resists police and vigilante murders. It is not an easy read. We will not all agree on its analyses or advocacy. Yet, its integrity, clarity, vulnerability, love and rage are clear. As a librarian who archives liberators and liberation movements, I recognize essential reading as a reflection of ourselves and our fears. With resolution, this text resonates with narratives of mini-Atticas. The 1971 prison rebellion and murderous repression by government and officialdom reveal the crises that spark radical movements and increasing calls for self-defense. This volume offers our cracked mirrors as an opportunity to scrutinize missteps and possibilities, and hopefully choose wisely even in our sacrifices."
—Joy James, author of *Resisting State Violence: Radicalism, Gender, and Race in U.S. Culture*

Anarchic Agreements: A Field Guide to Collective Organizing

Ruth Kinna, Alex Prichard, Thomas Swann, and Seeds for Change

ISBN: 978-1-62963-963-5
$15.95   112 pages

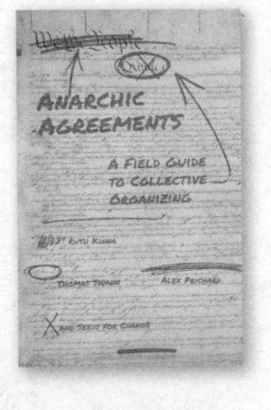

A new world is possible and not just in our hearts. *Anarchic Agreements* is a quintessential field guide for the revolution, answering the practical questions often left out of works of political theory and philosophy. How do leaderless groups organize? How might they create constitutions, balance power and write protocols? How do group cultures and institutions maintain coalitions? This urgent and inspiring how-to is the product of more than twenty years of research. Designed explicitly for everyday use, it contains lived examples and text from current horizontally organized constitutions. These documents illustrate the never-ending process of developing community and keeping collaborations alive in the fairest ways possible. Written by dedicated anarchist scholars and organizers, and based on the widely popular Anarchic Agreements pamphlet series, this book facilitates grassroots activism and provides methods to improve and streamline decision making. It is an inspiring celebration of the novel, complex, and flexible constitutions anarchists have created over time. This book shows how to realize another world, collectively without domination, while leaving the future open to infinite other possibilities.

"*Anarchic Agreements is a kind of how-to offering about something not often codified at all, much less with systematic and comprehensive care—forming effective groups, and then, groups of groups, consistently with anarchist aspirations and insights. It addresses the nitty gritty of working well together, a focus that everyone who wants a better world ought to prioritize.*"
—Michael Albert, ZNet, author of *Practical Utopia*

"*I've been using the tools and principles in the Anarchic Agreements pamphlets—here at last as one book, with more besides—since 2017. The book works with campaign groups, charities, housing co-ops, workers' co-ops, and all sorts of organisations and committees with an aspiration to be less hierarchical or to work better with volunteers. Making agreements that are consensual, changeable, and conscious is the keystone for making groups that last. It can also be a tonic for groups that have gone stale, inherited old rules, or need a new shared vocabulary to move from a vision of the future to the real thing.*"
—Jed Picksley, community organiser, trainer, activist, and permaculturist

We Go Where They Go: The Story of Anti-Racist Action

Shannon Clay, Lady, Kristin Schwartz, and Michael Staudenmaier with a Foreword by Gord Hill

ISBN: 978-1-62963-972-7 (paperback)
       978-1-62963-977-2 (hardcover)
$24.95/$59.95   320 pages

What does it mean to risk all for your beliefs? How do you fight an enemy in your midst? *We Go Where They Go* recounts the thrilling story of a massive forgotten youth movement that set the stage for today's anti-fascist organizing in North America. When skinheads and punks in the late 1980s found their communities invaded by white supremacists and neo-nazis, they fought back. Influenced by anarchism, feminism, Black liberation, and Indigenous sovereignty, they created Anti-Racist Action. At ARA's height in the 1990s, thousands of dedicated activists in hundreds of chapters joined the fights—political and sometimes physical—against nazis, the Ku Klux Klan, anti-abortion fundamentalists, and racist police. Before media pundits, cynical politicians, and your uncle discovered "antifa," Anti-Racist Action was bringing it to the streets.

Based on extensive interviews with dozens of ARA participants, *We Go Where They Go* tells ARA's story from within, giving voice to those who risked their safety in their own defense and in solidarity with others. In reproducing the posters, zines, propaganda and photos of the movement itself, this essential work of radical history illustrates how cultural scenes can become powerful forces for change. Here at last is the story of an organic yet highly organized movement, exploring both its triumphs and failures, and offering valuable lessons for today's generation of activists and rabble-rousers. *We Go Where They Go* is a page-turning history of grassroots anti-racism. More than just inspiration, it's a roadmap.

"I was a big supporter and it was an honor to work with the Anti-Racist Action movement. Their unapologetic and uncompromising opposition to racism and fascism in the streets, in the government, and in the mosh pit continues to be inspiring to this day."
—Tom Morello

"Antifa became a household word with Trump attempting and failing to designate it a domestic terrorist group, but Antifa's roots date back to the late 1980s when little attention was being paid to violent fascist groups that were flourishing under Reaganism, and Anti-Racist Action (ARA) was singular and effective in its brilliant offensive. This book tells the story of ARA in breathtaking prose accompanied by stunning photographs and images."
—Roxanne Dunbar-Ortiz, author of *Loaded: A Disarming History of the Second Amendment*

Mutual Aid: An Illuminated Factor of Evolution

Peter Kropotkin
Illustrated by N.O. Bonzo with an
Introduction by David Graeber & Andrej
Grubačić, Foreword by Ruth Kinna,
Postscript by GATS, and an Afterword
by Allan Antliff

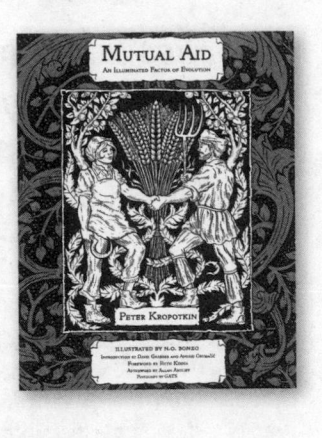

ISBN: 978-1-62963-874-4 (paperback)
       978-1-62963-875-1 (hardcover)
$30.00/$59.95   336 pages

One hundred years after his death, Peter Kropotkin is still one of the most inspirational figures of the anarchist movement. It is often forgotten that Kropotkin was also a world-renowned geographer whose seminal critique of the hypothesis of competition promoted by social Darwinism helped revolutionize modern evolutionary theory. An admirer of Darwin, he used his observations of life in Siberia as the basis for his 1902 collection of essays *Mutual Aid: A Factor of Evolution*. Kropotkin demonstrated that mutually beneficial cooperation and reciprocity—in both individuals and as a species—plays a far more important role in the animal kingdom and human societies than does individualized competitive struggle. Kropotkin carefully crafted his theory making the science accessible. His account of nature rejected Rousseau's romantic depictions and ethical socialist ideas that cooperation was motivated by the notion of "universal love." His understanding of the dynamics of social evolution shows us the power of cooperation—whether it is bison defending themselves against a predator or workers unionizing against their boss. His message is clear: solidarity is strength!

Every page of this new edition of *Mutual Aid* has been beautifully illustrated by one of anarchism's most celebrated current artists, N.O. Bonzo. The reader will also enjoy original artwork by GATS and insightful commentary by David Graeber, Ruth Kinna, Andrej Grubačić, and Allan Antliff.

"*N.O. Bonzo has created a rare document, updating Kropotkin's anarchist classic* Mutual Aid, *by intertwining compelling imagery with an updated text. Filled with illustrious examples, their art gives the words and histories, past and present, resonance for new generations to seed flowers of cooperation to push through the concrete of resistance to show liberatory possibilities for collective futures.*"
—scott crow, author of *Black Flags and Windmills* and *Setting Sights*

"*Taking aim at both social Darwinists and Romantic dreamers, Kropotkin's classic text makes plain that the promise of liberation arises from our collective instinct to cooperate. In this new edition, lovingly illuminated by N.O. Bonzo, we can see the powerful amplifying effect of mutual aid firsthand.*"
—AK Thompson, author of *Black Bloc, White Riot*

Wobblies and Zapatistas: Conversations on Anarchism, Marxism and Radical History

Staughton Lynd and Andrej Grubačić

ISBN: 978-1-60486-041-2
$20.00   300 pages

Wobblies and Zapatistas offers the reader an encounter between two generations and two traditions. Andrej Grubačić is an anarchist from the Balkans. Staughton Lynd is a lifelong pacifist, influenced by Marxism. They meet in dialogue in an effort to bring together the anarchist and Marxist traditions, to discuss the writing of history by those who make it, and to remind us of the idea that "my country is the world." Encompassing a Left libertarian perspective and an emphatically activist standpoint, these conversations are meant to be read in the clubs and affinity groups of the new Movement.

The authors accompany us on a journey through modern revolutions, direct actions, anti-globalist counter summits, Freedom Schools, Zapatista cooperatives, Haymarket and Petrograd, Hanoi and Belgrade, 'intentional' communities, wildcat strikes, early Protestant communities, Native American democratic practices, the Workers' Solidarity Club of Youngstown, occupied factories, self-organized councils and soviets, the lives of forgotten revolutionaries, Quaker meetings, antiwar movements, and prison rebellions. Neglected and forgotten moments of interracial self-activity are brought to light. The book invites the attention of readers who believe that a better world, on the other side of capitalism and state bureaucracy, may indeed be possible.

"There's no doubt that we've lost much of our history. It's also very clear that those in power in this country like it that way. Here's a book that shows us why. It demonstrates not only that another world is possible, but that it already exists, has existed, and shows an endless potential to burst through the artificial walls and divisions that currently imprison us. An exquisite contribution to the literature of human freedom, and coming not a moment too soon."
—David Graeber, author of *Fragments of an Anarchist Anthropology* and *Direct Action: An Ethnography*

"I have been in regular contact with Andrej Grubačić for many years, and have been most impressed by his searching intelligence, broad knowledge, lucid judgment, and penetrating commentary on contemporary affairs and their historical roots. He is an original thinker and dedicated activist, who brings deep understanding and outstanding personal qualities to everything he does."
—Noam Chomsky

No Harmless Power: The Life and Times of the Ukrainian Anarchist Nestor Makhno

Charlie Allison
Illustrated by Kevin Matthews and
N.O. Bonzo

ISBN: 978-1-62963-471-5
$21.95   256 pages

Lively, incendiary, and inspiring, *No Harmless Power*
follows the life of Nestor Makhno, who organized a seven-million-strong anarchist
polity during the Russian Civil War and developed Platformist anarchism during
his exile in Paris as well as advising other anarchists like Durruti on tactics and
propaganda. Both timely and timeless, this biography reveals Makhno's rapidly
changing world and his place in it. He moved swiftly from peasant youth to
prisoner to revolutionary anarchist leader, narrowly escaping Bolshevik Ukraine
for Paris. This book also chronicles the friends and enemies he made along the
way: Lenin, Trotsky, Kropotkin, Alexander Berkman, Emma Goldman, Ida Mett, and
others.

No Harmless Power is the first text to fully delve into Makhno's sympathy for the
downtrodden, the trap of personal heroism, his improbable victories, unlikely
friendships, and his alarming lack of gun safety in meetings. Makhno and the
movement he began are seldom mentioned in most mainstream histories—
Western or Russian—mostly on the grounds that acknowledging anarchist polities
calls into question the inevitability and desirability of the nation-state and unjust
hierarchies.

With illustrations by N.O. Bonzo and Kevin Matthews, this is a fresh, humorous,
and necessary look at an under examined corner of history as well as a deep
exploration of the meaning—and value, if any—of heroism as history.

*"A biography that reads like a great adventure story, this tale of freedom-fighting and
myth-making in early-twentieth-century Eastern Europe is as entertaining as it is
necessary."*
—Stephanie Feldman, author of *Angel of Losses* and *Saturnalia*

*"Charles Allison has turned his talents to a topic that was colorful and interesting even
before recent global events gave Ukraine fresh relevance. Allison's accessible and
humorous writing saturates the book with passages that are chock-full of the sort of
informational nuggets that readers will enjoy passing along to friends and family."*
—Matt Hongoltz-Hetling, author of *A Libertarian Walks into a Bear: The Utopian Plot
to Liberate an American Town (and Some Bears)*

Their Blood Got Mixed: Revolutionary Rojava and the War on ISIS

Janet Biehl

ISBN: 978-1-62963-944-4
$27.95   256 pages

In the summer of 2012 the Kurdish people of northern Syria set out to create a multiethnic society in the Middle East. Persecuted for much of the 20th century, they dared to try to overcome social fragmentation by affirming social solidarity among all the region's ethnic and religious peoples. As Syria plunged into civil war, the Kurds and their Arab and Assyrian allies established a self-governing polity that was not only multiethnic but democratic. And women were not only permitted but encouraged to participate in all social roles alongside men, including political and military roles.

To implement these goals, Rojava wanted to live in peace with its neighbors. Instead, it soon faced invasion by ISIS, a force that was in every way its opposite. ISIS attacked its neighbors in Iraq and Syria, imposing theocratic, tyrannical, femicidal rule on them. Those who might have resisted fled in terror. But when ISIS attacked the mostly Kurdish city of Kobane and overran much of it, the YPG and YPJ, or people's militias, declined to flee. Instead they resisted, and several countries, seeing their valiant resistance, formed an international coalition to assist them militarily. While the YPG and YPJ fought on the ground, the coalition coordinated airstrikes with them. They liberated village after village and in March 2019 captured ISIS's last territory in Syria.

Around that time, two UK-based filmmakers invited the author to spend a month in Rojava making a film. She accepted, and arrived to explore the society and interview people. During that month, she explored how the revolution had progressed and especially the effects of the war on the society. She found that the war had reinforced social solidarity and welded together the multiethnic, gender-liberated society. As one man in Kobane told her, "Our blood got mixed."

"You haven't been to Rojava yet? Let Janet Biehl's graphic novel help you take your first step to the land of revolutionary hope, to North-East Syria, by providing a fascinating glimpse and thrilling insight into the most significant revolution of the 21st century. History is usually written by powerful elites and rulers, but Janet Biehl invites us to a new viewpoint. Their Blood Got Mixed is a creative contribution to a historiography from the perspective of those who actually made it."
—Havin Guneser, one of the spokespersons of the International Initiative "Freedom for Abdullah Öcalan—Peace in Kurdistan" and author of *The Art of Freedom*

Zapatista Stories for Dreaming Another World

Subcomandante Marcos
Edited and translated by Colectivo
Relámpago/Lightning Collective with a
Foreword by JoAnn Wypijewski

ISBN: 978-1-62963-970-3
$16.95   160 pages

In this gorgeous collection of allegorical stories, Subcomandante Marcos, idiosyncratic spokesperson of the Zapatistas, has provided "an accidental archive" of a revolutionary group's struggle against neoliberalism. For thirty years, the Zapatistas have influenced and inspired movements worldwide, showing that another world is possible. They have infused left politics with a distinct imaginary—and an imaginative, literary, or poetic dimension—organizing horizontally, outside and against the state, and with a profound respect for difference as a source of political insight, not division. With commentaries that illuminate their historical, political, and literary contexts and an introduction by the translators, this timeless, elegiac volume is perfect for lovers of literature and lovers of revolution.

"From the beating heart of Mesoamerica the old gods speak to Old Antonio, a glasses-wearing, pipe-smoking beetle who studies neoliberalism, and both tell their tales to Subcomandante Marcos who passes them on to us: the stories of the Zapatistas' revolutionary struggles from below and to the left. The Colectivo Relámpago (Lightning Collective), based in Amherst, Massachusetts, translates and comments with bolts of illumination zigzagging across cultures and nations, bringing bursts of laughter and sudden charges of hot-wired political energy. It seems like child's play, yet it's almost divine!"
—Peter Linebaugh, author of Red Round Globe Hot Burning

"This is a beautiful, inspired project. In a joyful Zapatista gesture readers will welcome, this volume invites us to play, to walk on different, and even contrary paths through smooth and crystalline translations that bring these 'other stories' to life. The translators' commentaries preserve a delicate balance of expertise and autonomy as they illuminate the historical, political, and cultural forces that provoked the stories' creation. Among these forces are Zapatista women, whom the translators rightly dignify in their meticulous and provocative introduction. This volume is a gift to so many of us as we (attempt to) bring the Zapatista imagination to our students and organizing communities."
—Michelle Joffroy, associate professor of Spanish and Latin American & Latino Studies, Smith College and co-director of Domestic Workers Make History

Anarchy in Action

Colin Ward

ISBN: 978-1-62963-238-4
$15.95   192 pages

The argument of this book is that an anarchist society,
a society which organizes itself without authority, is
always in existence, like a seed beneath the snow,
buried under the weight of the state and its bureaucracy,
capitalism and its waste, privilege and its injustices,
nationalism and its suicidal loyalties, religious
differences and their superstitious separatism.

Anarchist ideas are so much at variance with ordinary political assumptions and
the solutions anarchists offer so remote, that all too often people find it hard to
take anarchism seriously. This classic text is an attempt to bridge the gap between
the present reality and anarchist aspirations, "between what is and what, according
to the anarchists, might be."

Through a wide-ranging analysis—drawing on examples from education, urban
planning, welfare, housing, the environment, the workplace, and the family, to
name but a few—Colin Ward demonstrates that the roots of anarchist practice are
not so alien or quixotic as they might at first seem but lie precisely in the ways that
people have always tended to organize themselves when left alone to do so. The
result is both an accessible introduction for those new to anarchism and pause for
thought for those who are too quick to dismiss it.

For more than thirty years, in over thirty books, Colin Ward patiently explained
anarchist solutions to everything from vandalism to climate change—and
celebrated unofficial uses of the landscape as commons, from holiday camps to
squatter communities. Ward was an anarchist journalist and editor for almost sixty
years, most famously editing the journal *Anarchy*. He was also a columnist for *New
Statesman*, *New Society*, *Freedom*, and *Town and Country Planning*.

*"It is difficult to match the empirical strength, the lucidity of prose, and the integration
of theory and practical insight in the magnificent body of work produced by the veteran
anarchist Colin Ward."*
—*Prospect*

*"Colin Ward has never written a highly paid column for a national newspaper or been
on the bestseller lists, but his fan club is distinguished, and his influence wider than he
himself may know."*
—*Times Literary Supplement*

Beyond State, Power, and Violence

Abdullah Öcalan
with a Foreword by Andrej Grubačić
Edited by International Initiative

ISBN: 978-1-62963-715-0
$29.95   800 pages

After the dissolution of the PKK (Kurdistan Workers' Party) in 2002, internal discussions ran high, and fear and uncertainty about the future of the Kurdish freedom movement threatened to unravel the gains of decades of organizing and armed struggle. From his prison cell, Abdullah Öcalan intervened by penning his most influential work to date: *Beyond State, Power, and Violence*. With a stunning vision of a freedom movement centered on women's liberation, democracy, and ecology, Öcalan helped reinvigorate the Kurdish freedom movement by providing a revolutionary path forward with what is undoubtedly the furthest-reaching definition of democracy the world has ever seen. Here, for the first time, is the highly anticipated English translation of this monumental work.

Beyond State, Power, and Violence is a breathtaking reconnaissance into life without the state, an essential portrait of the PKK and the Kurdish freedom movement, and an open blueprint for leftist organizing in the twenty-first century, written by one of the most vitally important political luminaries of today.

By carefully analyzing the past and present of the Middle East, Öcalan evaluates concrete prospects for the Kurdish people and arrives with his central proposal: recreate the Kurdish freedom movement along the lines of a new paradigm based on the principles of democratic confederalism and democratic autonomy. In the vast scope of this book, Öcalan examines the emergence of hierarchies and eventually classes in human societies and sketches his alternative, the democratic-ecological society. This vision, with a theoretical foundation of a nonviolent means of taking power, has ushered in a new era for the Kurdish freedom movement while also offering a fresh and indispensible perspective on the global debate about a new socialism. Öcalan's calls for nonhierarchical forms of democratic social organization deserve the careful attention of anyone interested in constructive social thought or rebuilding society along feminist and ecological lines.

"Öcalan's works make many intellectuals uncomfortable because they represent a form of thought which is not only inextricable from action, but which directly grapples with the knowledge that it is."
—David Graeber author of *Debt: The First 500 Years*

Liberating Sápmi: Indigenous Resistance in Europe's Far North

Gabriel Kuhn

ISBN: 978-1-62963-712-9
$17.00   220 pages

The Sámi, who have inhabited Europe's far north for thousands of years, are often referred to as the continent's "forgotten people." With Sápmi, their traditional homeland, divided between four nation-states—Norway, Sweden, Finland, and Russia—the Sámi have experienced the profound oppression and discrimination that characterize the fate of indigenous people worldwide: their lands have been confiscated, their beliefs and values attacked, their communities and families torn apart. Yet the Sámi have shown incredible resilience, defending their identity and their territories and retaining an important social and ecological voice—even if many, progressives and leftists included, refuse to listen.

Liberating Sápmi is a stunning journey through Sápmi and includes in-depth interviews with Sámi artists, activists, and scholars boldly standing up for the rights of their people. In this beautifully illustrated work, Gabriel Kuhn, author of over a dozen books and our most fascinating interpreter of global social justice movements, aims to raise awareness of the ongoing fight of the Sámi for justice and self-determination. The first accessible English-language introduction to the history of the Sámi people and the first account that focuses on their political resistance, this provocative work gives irrefutable evidence of the important role the Sámi play in the resistance of indigenous people against an economic and political system whose power to destroy all life on earth has reached a scale unprecedented in the history of humanity.

The book contains interviews with Mari Boine, Harald Gaski, Ann-Kristin Håkansson, Aslak Holmberg, Maxida Märak, Stefan Mikaelsson, May-Britt Öhman, Synnøve Persen, Øyvind Ravna, Niillas Somby, Anders Sunna, and Suvi West.

"I'm highly recommending Gabriel Kuhn's book Liberating Sápmi *to anyone seeking to understand the world of today through indigenous eyes. Kuhn concisely and dramatically opens our eyes to little-known Sápmi history, then in the perfect follow-up brings us up to date with a unique collection of interviews with a dozen of today's most brilliant contemporary Sámi voices. Bravo."*
—Buffy Sainte-Marie, Cree, singer-songwriter